# Advance
## Slow

"This book is exactly what I needed. I'm tired of the 'hustle and grind' mentality of most motivational goal-setting books and programs. Stephanie's down-to-earth style helped me realize I could still reach my dreams and goals but with a gentler approach that didn't leave me feeling behind the pack. Her steady, slow, and sustainable guidance is the message I'd been craving."

— Kim Demmon, founder of *Today's Creative Life*

"A treasure. In a world where every social force urges us to speed up and think faster and do faster, Stephanie O'Dea shows us how to slow down for better, smarter, happier living."

— *New York Times* bestselling author
Zac Bissonnette

"Fantastic resource for college and postgraduate students, and folks in the throes of life: kids, careers, and trying to juggle all of it—anyone looking to live a more intentional life."

— Laurie Palau, founder of Simply B Organized
and host of *This Organized Life* podcast

"This is a perfect book if you are overworked, overwhelmed, and in need of guidance to change your lifestyle and learn routines to live a life with peace, meaning, and balance."

— Susan Sawczuk, elementary school educator
of over twenty-five years

"Stephanie O'Dea pushes back against Hustle Culture as a pervasive norm and shows us a better way. *Slow Living* is a road map for living well, and Steph is our sensible, compassionate guide. In this book, she encapsulates her decades of wisdom and experience into one manual offering accessible, actionable 'teeny-tiny baby steps.'"

— Sandy Cooper, fellow anti-hustle advocate, host
of *The Balanced MomCast* and *Writing Off Social*,
and author of three books

"*Slow Living* is an excellent guide to living honestly, authentically, and bravely in this ever-changing, dynamic world, in which we must be vigilant and deliberate about protecting what matters most and not seduced by a superficial existence. If you are ready to do the meaningful work, *Slow Living* is a great place to embark upon your journey within."

— Dr. Emily Bashah, licensed clinical psychologist,
author of *Addictive Ideologies: Finding Meaning and
Agency When Politics Fail You,* and co-host of the
*Optimistic American* podcast

"Through these pages, Stephanie O'Dea will gently and beautifully lead you on the path of building your very best life. The relatable moments from her own journey will help you see yourself moving into the Slow Living world she so wonderfully describes. The acronyms she uses in her own life will become the structure for you as you develop and implement these principles into your life. Along the way, you'll redefine FOMO, go to PROM in your own home, and set the GPS and new PACE of your life. The words, frameworks, and exercises in this book will be a healing balm to your mind, heart, and soul."

— Erin Chase, cookbook author and founder of
$5 Dinners

# Slow Living

## Cultivating a Life of Purpose in a Hustle-Driven World

by Stephanie O'Dea

DEXTERITY
NASHVILLE

604 Magnolia Lane
Nashville, TN 37211

Scripture quotations marked KJV are taken from the King James Version of the Bible. Public domain.

Printed in the United States of America

First edition: 2024

10 9 8 7 6 5 4 3 2 1

ISBN: 978-1-962435-07-9 (Paperback)
ISBN: 978-1-962435-08-6 (E-book)
ISBN: 978-1-962435-09-3 (Audiobook)

Publisher's Cataloging-in-Publication data

Names: O'Dea, Stephanie, Mae, 1976–, author.
Title: Slow living : cultivating a life of purpose in a hustle-driven world / Stephanie O'Dea.
Description: Includes bibliographical references. | Nashville, TN: Dexterity, 2024.
Identifiers: ISBN: 978-1-962435-07-9 (paperback) | 978-1-962435-08-6 (ebook) | 978-1-962435-09-3 (audio)
Subjects: LCSH Conduct of life. | Self-actualization (Psychology). | Simplicity. | Self-help. | Self-help techniques. | BISAC SELF-HELP. / Personal Growth / General. | SELF-HELP. / Motivational & Inspirational. | BODY, MIND, & SPIRIT. / Inspiration & Personal Growth Classification: LCC BJ1589.O34 2024 | DDC 158–dc23

Interior design by Lapiz Digital.

*To my three baby girls:*

*I love you.*
*I'm proud of you.*
*And I think you are wonderful.*

# Contents

# Preface

# Create the Life You've Always Wanted

Dear Reader,

I'm so glad you're here. This book has been percolating in the back of my mind for roughly twenty-five years, and now that my own children are entering their adult years, I figured it was time to finally write it all down.

This book is the how-to guide for life that I wish I had when, new to adulthood, I realized that after following carefully outlined syllabi for my schooling for years, there wasn't a similar daily, weekly, or monthly agenda for adulting.

And I desperately wanted one.

I wanted someone, somewhere to tell me that I was on the right path and that if I just kept going, all of my hopes, dreams, and wishes would eventually come to fruition. I wanted a fairy godmother of sorts to hold my hand and tell me that the anxious and nervous feelings were normal, and that there really wasn't anyone doing it "better" than I was.

It also was super important to me that I not be told to do more than I was already doing. I already felt as if my days were filled with all of the things that had to get done, and that there wasn't enough time for the things that I really wanted to do—like reading, yoga, napping, spending time in nature, and putting together puzzles with my family.

I wanted reassurance that my endless research and insomnia-filled nights scrolling online for been-there-done-that advice wasn't in vain, and that if I just took a deep breath and trusted my inner gut I'd turn out okay, and so would my children. Even if we didn't have the newest and flashiest gadgets or wear expensive clothes in luxurious vacation settings, we would be okay. Heck, some of our favorite memories are of camping trips when it poured on us and we all huddled in the tent trailer to keep warm!

So I started writing.

Actually, before that, I started the *Slow Living* podcast and began coaching. Through the podcast and my coaching work, it became clear how many people were craving a non-hustling approach to life.

I also wasn't the only one who longed for a simpler time where the days felt long and meandering and there wasn't a constant pressure to perform better or faster or cram more into an already overflowing day.

I found an entire community of people, just like me, who wanted to live slowly.

We didn't want to be told that we were "doing it wrong" for not wanting to do things faster or better or with more technology. We didn't want to watch our children grow up through the lens of a smartphone camera, but instead wanted to be fully present and soak in the ups and downs of life. Mostly, we wanted reassurance that we would get to our goal even if we took the meandering cobblestone path instead of the highway.

That's what Slow Living is all about, and that is why I felt so compelled to write this book.

But first, I'm going to tell you something that most self-help and how-to authors won't—you don't *need* this book.

You don't need me either. I'm not going to unveil the secret of the Universe or unlock a vault full of riches and the key to success.

Growing up, one of my favorite family memories was watching *The Wizard of Oz* on TV each year around Thanksgiving. The first few times I watched the movie, I was scared of some of the imagery, but as I grew into an older teen, I paid closer attention to the dialogue and central theme.

First published in 1900, *The Wonderful Wizard of Oz* was written by L. Frank Baum. The story opens with the main character, Dorothy Gale, a young girl in Kansas, being swept away to the magical land of Oz in a tornado. In 1939, the book was adapted into the movie, which was directed by Victor Fleming and starred Judy Garland as Dorothy.

The story follows Dorothy as she follows the path laid out before her (the iconic yellow brick road) and meets various characters (the Scarecrow, Tin Man, and Cowardly Lion) who advise her on how she can leave Oz to return home to Kansas. At the conclusion of the story, it's revealed to Dorothy that she actually didn't need to follow the advice or suggestions, because she had the power to return home all on her own.

My hope for you, through reading this book and participating in the suggested exercises, is that you'll explore within, begin to believe in yourself and your decision-making process, and trust that just like Dorothy in *The Wizard of Oz*, you have the answers already.

If you'd like some guidance on this journey, I'm here for you! For years, I have helped busy people create the lives they've always dreamt about, from the ground up, by building a solid foundation of success that encapsulates all aspects of life: time management, health, finances, organization, and relationships. This book simplifies decades of my research and study of personal development, self-discovery, and spiritual texts and teachings into bite-sized, actionable chunks that you can start implementing immediately to make long-lasting changes for the better in your everyday life.

"Dream big." "Visualize your future." "Figure out your purpose." We've all heard these well-meaning phrases, handed down by self-help and personal development teachers, advisors, and gurus. But for those of us with practical, analytical, or somewhat skeptical brains, it's quite difficult to see how daydreaming and envisioning your future can result in tangible results.

On the flip side, it can be rather disheartening to feel as if you're getting yelled at for not working hard enough at life or for sometimes thinking self-sabotaging thoughts.

Guess what? You aren't a robot, and in real life, humans think hundreds of thousands of thoughts each day—some of them negative.

It's impossible to believe you can control all your thoughts, and anyone who preaches that you can completely erase all human suffering and natural disasters by simply "thinking better" isn't being honest. So how *can* you drastically change your life for the better? Even change the world around you? By being thoughtful and methodical and by taking teeny-tiny baby steps forward in each aspect of your life, every day.

I strongly believe that we do not live in a one-size-fits-all world, but if you are looking for a formula to stick onto your refrigerator or write in your journal, it's this: Mindset + Action + Consistency = Success.

I have broken this formula into bite-sized pieces in this book, organized within four sections. I include the exact steps I use with my clients to thoughtfully change the trajectory of their lives for the better, including practical and time-tested advice that spans socioeconomic segments.

### Part 1—Mindset: The Why

In this first part, we will define Slow Living and explain how purposefully slowing down and stepping away from Hustle Culture is the key to long-term success. I will also lay out how to "step into" a thought that feels good as you move toward your goals in a purposeful way.

### Part 2—The Five Steps to Slow Living: The How

This second section teaches the step-by-step approach to creating a slow, steady, and sustainable life in a way that feels good to you. If you're looking for checklists and a paint-by-numbers guide, this is it.

### Part 3—The Peace Pyramid: The Reward

In this part, we will apply the action steps learned in Part 2 to every portion of your life. After taking the time to lay the foundational components of your life in a thoughtful and sustainable way, you'll begin to feel a sense of peace and purpose—which is the fun part of a life well-lived!

### Part 4—Walking It Out: The Journey

In this section, you'll learn that the things you do every day define you. You'll also learn practical ways to keep moving forward in a consistent way toward your goals and dream life through the ups, downs, and all-arounds of real life.

If you're ready to stop spinning your wheels and start creating the life you've always wanted, join me! Together, we will slowly and sustainably build the life of your dreams, step-by-step, brick-by-brick.

## A Note About Privilege

I'd like to acknowledge the privileges that have shaped my perspective and how they have created blind spots and biases. I have made a conscious effort to examine my own privilege throughout my work and in this book.

- I grew up in the suburbs. I was fortunate to live in a safe, comfortable environment that offered access to quality education, healthcare, and opportunities.
- My parents have been married for over fifty years, which provided a stable, safe, and supportive family structure alongside emotional and financial security.
- I graduated from college without student loans. Not everyone is able to pursue higher education, especially without the burden of student debt.
- I am Caucasian, which has afforded me the privilege of not having to contend with systemic racism.
- I am heterosexual and identify with the gender I was assigned at birth, which spares me the challenges and prejudices faced by those who identify differently.

I strive to be empathetic and inclusive in my storytelling and perspectives. My goal is to promote inclusivity and empathy as we explore long-term personal and professional goals in a slow, steady, and sustainable way. Thank you for being here, and please consider yourself loved and hugged. I think you are wonderful.

XOXO,

Steph

# Introduction

# The Joy of Slowing Down

What if I told you that you can truly "have it all"—work, family, social life, financial independence, and health—all working together in a cohesive way?

You might tell me I'm out to lunch, and I wouldn't blame you. I feel like I've been lied to and overpromised this multiple times as well.

The self-help and personal development books I grew up reading, and those your parents and grandparents referred to, may have worked in the past, but the advice now reads a bit tone-deaf and far-fetched, and they certainly are not playbooks for today's structures.

"Do What You Love and the Money will Follow" is outdated and broken. Another fan favorite—"Go to College, Get a Good Job, Work Hard, Retire"—also seems unrealistic. This doesn't mean that you can't live a successful life. But it does mean that holding your breath and hoping that following worn-out advice will somehow magically result in all your dreams coming true isn't a recipe for success.

People who subscribe to the notion that "you need to keep your nose to the grindstone" will always claim that you didn't work hard enough if you didn't achieve all that you wanted out of life. Guess what? It's not all that motivating to be told you're doing life wrong and that it's all your fault that you aren't living what others call a "successful" life!

I don't know about you, but for me, the idea that you are only allowed to feel successful if you're in the "Work Hard, Play Hard" camp seems an exhausting way to live. How fun can it be to wear yourself thin, only to have a few days off here and there for vacation and relaxation?

Another method many self-help and personal development authors advocate is to wish, hope, pray, and trust that God or the Universe will deliver all you could possibly want in life if you think certain thoughts or meditate in a specific way.

If you're reading this book, you've probably discovered (as I have) that none of the approaches described above have worked for you. So, what is "the secret sauce" to a life well-lived? How can you actually get from where you are right now to where you want to go? That's what we're going to cover in the chapters ahead.

It all starts with learning how to Slow Down.

I promise you that you can still dream big and follow a path to your own definition of a life well-lived. Many people lament that the American Dream is dead. It may have shifted and changed a bit to better reflect today's beliefs and desires, but it's not dead. The secret is to really look inside of yourself and decide what *you* want—not what society or capitalism tells you that you want or need.

Success in life doesn't equal believing differently or working harder. It also doesn't necessarily look like living in a mansion with 2.3 children and a golden retriever behind a white picket fence.

And where you are right now isn't your fault, or society's fault, or your parents' fault. It just is what it is. You don't need to do a deep dive to figure out what experiences or life events caused you to be the way you are. Instead, just become aware of where you are and where you want to go. Together, we will map out a plan to get you from here to there.

You are not behind if you haven't figured it all out already or if you secretly worry that you're on the wrong path. Most people feel this way at various times in life, and this is what differentiates humans from other large-brained mammals. I'd ask that instead of dismissing change and growth as impossible or not applicable for you and your current life experience—remain curious. As we go through the exercises in this book, together we can work to better your life.

You are not alone, and there is time to course-correct.

I'm so happy you're here.

> **"Be thankful for what you have; you'll end up having more. If you concentrate on what you don't have, you will never, ever have enough."**
> **—Oprah Winfrey**

## How This All Started

I'd like to say right off the bat that *I am no one special*. I do feel as if I'm living the life of my dreams, but I am not special. I don't have a bunch of letters after my name.

I'm a mom of three girls and a basset hound named Sheldon. I married my high school sweetheart, and we live in the suburbs in a normal house and live a normal life.

I used to write cookbooks and am currently a life coach and podcaster who also works in the front office of an elementary school.

I'm best known professionally for my A Year of Slow Cooking website, which I started on a whim as a New Year's resolution in 2008 to use my slow cooker every day for a year and write about it online.

This simple idea resulted in four cookbooks, including a coveted spot on the *New York Times* Best Sellers list, multiple television appearances, and a highly visited website that garnered up to $1,000 a day in banner ads. At one point, the website I built on my own, in my pajamas, with no money down, was declared the number three food blog in the United States by PR firm Cision.[1]

I started the website because I wanted a legitimate way to make money online while staying home to care for my children. And I loved the lifestyle I was able to create. I worked on my website in the early mornings while my young children slept, and I had plenty of time during the day to volunteer in their classrooms and visit with my grandparents.

While I really enjoyed many aspects of my time as a food writer, I didn't actually like the writing-only-about-food part.

I have always liked to write and teach, and the best part of my day was waking up early to answer questions emailed from readers from all over the world. Once I realized that the questions were more about life and time management than about slow cooking, I decided to get certified as a life coach and began recording episodes of the *Slow Living* podcast.

I had gotten my start in coaching and working with families at a childcare center housed within a homeless shelter before I had children of my own. Part of my job was to help teach parenting classes and map out a three-to-five-year life plan for the people who lived there.

I still use the training and teachings I learned from that experience over two decades ago to shape and guide my writing and coaching today.

Thanks to the schoolwork and classes I took to become certified in Early Childhood Education, while also obtaining a bachelor's in English literature from San Francisco State University, I became entrenched in the concept of the "teachable moment." It applied to working with young kids as well as their parents. Often, I'd have to scrap the planned daily lesson because a teachable moment presented itself.

I loved being able to stop on a dime, switch a lever in my brain, and guide the children and parents I worked with during these teachable moments.

This book grew out of one such teachable moment during the slowdown the entire world experienced amid the Covid-19 lockdowns in 2020. The work I did over those initial months of the pandemic (which turned into years) shined a light on what people were seeking out of life—and most of them were *not* seeking more.

Instead, over these past twenty-odd years working with (primarily) women and families, I've learned that most humans are trying to simplify their lives and really only want to achieve a feeling of inner peace and harmony—a sense of happiness.

A confident feeling that all the things they "had to do" were taken care of so they could finally do the things that they "wanted to do."

Most people want to do things like:

• garden
• read
• do yoga
• write
• take naps
• scrapbook
• paint
• take a photography class

In a nutshell, most of the people that I speak to and interview aren't interested in learning how to cram more into an already overflowing day. They're tired of headlines insinuating that they aren't doing enough. Instead, people crave ways to Slow Down and truly enjoy the life they're building and the simple pleasures it holds.

I want this for you.

It's not fun to feel as if you're behind or are racing to cross the next thing off a very long to-do list. This doesn't mean that you shouldn't have goals or lists. I'm a huge proponent of taking the time to plan out your dreams in bite-sized goals, but I don't want you to think that happiness and inner peace are on the other side of your to-do list; they can be yours while you're *in* the process of reaching for your dreams.

What if you took the time to enjoy the process?

Isn't it nicer to Slow Down and look around while on your morning walk instead of powering through to burn the most calories in the shortest amount of time? You'll still get to your destination. Slow Down. Enjoy the process. Play and have fun *while* you continue to move forward on your goals. What's the point of chasing a personal or professional milestone if you alienate your friends and family in the process or neglect your physical or mental health?

I'd like you to take a deep breath in right now. As you exhale, release any preconceived notions you may have about what goal setting and achieving look like. You may need to do this multiple times throughout the book. Because whatever ideas or advice you may have heard, there is no one-size-fits-all approach to life planning. You need to determine what works for *you*, and you only.

Instead of adding to your to-do list, I'd like you to set it aside and embrace your inner three-year-old, and for every goal you set from here on out ask yourself, *Why?* When you take the time to ask yourself open-ended questions, your subconscious will bubble up with answers.

And that's what Slow Living is all about.

I've been a huge fan of acronyms ever since I was a child and my grandfather explained that the word *snafu* was a military acronym for Situation Normal, All ****ed Up. The idea that a bad word could be hiding within an everyday term was such an exciting and fascinating notion for my young mind that I've spent many hours ever since making up acronyms when I've been bored or stuck in a situation I can't get out of—such as a never-ending meeting or a long flight.

I will share with you quite a few acronyms in this book, and if you come up with any of your own, please let me know. I can't seem to get enough of them!

One of my favorite acronyms I've created is for the word SLOW:

**S**imply
**L**ook
**O**nly
**W**ithin

## Faster Does Not Equal Better

"There's too much to do and not enough time to do it!" Sound familiar? People from all over the world, from all walks of life, mutter these words to themselves, to close family and friends, and even to strangers on the internet each and every day.

Even though we have invented self-driving cars and found hacks and shortcuts to many of the world's problems and inconveniences, we still haven't found a way to add more time to our jam-packed days.

How on earth are you supposed to keep your home dust-bunny free, your refrigerator stocked with only organic produce, your marriage in check, fit into your skinny jeans, be your kids' best friend, continue to make progress on your professional goals, drink a gallon of water a day, keep in touch with friends and out-of-town family, and sleep for eight hours a night?

Just thinking about all of the things we "should" be doing is utterly exhausting.

Everywhere you turn in today's fast-paced world, you see headlines urging you to "Do More" and "Be Better" and "Achieve All You Can."

If you follow the headlines online and in magazines, it seems like living an average life is no longer an option. You either need to be the best, or not even bother trying. Is that what we want for ourselves? For our children?

*Health, Wealth, and the Pursuit of Happiness.* These words are usually synonymous with the definition of the American Dream, and how our country was built. Taken from the original statement Thomas Jefferson wrote into the *Declaration of Independence*, which was "life, liberty, and the pursuit of happiness," most historical scholars agree that the original sentiment was that each colonist should have the fundamental right to exist, the freedom to live according to their own wishes, and the ability to seek personal fulfillment with the idea that the government would protect and uphold these rights.

But somehow over the past 250 years (almost), this idea morphed into GO GO GO and MORE MORE MORE and the notion that in order to live a successful life, you need to be the BEST.

Not adequate. Not sufficient. The Best.

And quite frankly, it's killing us.

According to the National Institute of Mental Health, one in five adults in the US report issues of mental illness, and suicide is the second leading cause of death among twenty-five- to thirty-four-year-olds (after unintentional injury).[2]

Let's think about this. When did becoming The Best become a thing that we should all strive for? Who decided that the best is the best, and who decides what the best even is?

I remember when my oldest child was about six or seven and she had just finished a season playing in AYSO (the American Youth Soccer Organization), which has the motto "Everyone Plays." When her coach handed out a plastic trophy with her name on it, a dad from the back of the pack of assembled parents muttered, "Oh, great, participation trophies."

I shuddered a bit. I'm A-OK with participation trophies. You show up, try your darnedest, run around with your teammates on a sunny day, and get to eat orange slices. And then at the end of twelve weeks, you get to collect your trophy. That sounds pretty awesome!

Why wouldn't we want to boost our children's self-esteem in this way? Why wouldn't we as a society reward commitment and teamwork? Why wouldn't we celebrate having fun just for the sake of having fun? Why should only the top scorer get a trophy?

This is never so apparent as when our children are in high school and are preparing to apply to college. Straight As, a 4.0, are no longer considered The Best, since we now have AP exams and extra classes that can bump GPAs (grade point averages) well into the 4.6 and 4.7 range. Not only are grades inflated, but students are also forced to prove that they are "well-rounded," so they're pushed by well-meaning parents and academic advisors into taking music, language, and art classes in which they may have no interest.

It is not unusual for an anxious parent to ask how to best support their child to attend Stanford at their second-grade parent–teacher conference.

And I get it. We all want our children to succeed in life, but I think we can all agree that "your child's path to Stanford" is not what needs to be discussed for most second graders who are still mastering the art of tying shoes and not eating boogers.

So, let's pause here for a bit and Slow Down.

If you walk down the street, any street, and take a random poll, I'd venture to guess that practically all parents will respond "healthy and happy" when asked what they want out of life for their children.

Yes. The simple basics. So how did we get to this fast-paced "winner takes all" lifestyle that society is currently pushing?

## Rejecting Hustle Culture

Through my writing, coaching, and speaking, I have spoken with thousands of people, and the majority say that while they want to Slow Down their lives and the lives of their children, they are worried that they'll somehow be passed by when it comes to progress at work, financial abundance, and security for their children.

This is understandable.

That's because you're constantly being sold the story that what you have isn't good enough and that you should want and strive for something bigger, better, faster, shinier, and more expensive.

In fact, I once overheard parents chatting in the bleachers at a high school track event saying, "Second is the first loser."

Ouch!

Quite simply, it's easier to sell stuff to those who are unhappy. And marketers and the media and the ad execs on Madison Avenue all spend an awful lot of time, energy, and resources to keep you dissatisfied.

Unhappy with your current physical appearance? Buy this new exercise equipment, pop this pill, buy a whole new wardrobe, or pay for liposuction. Unhappy with your home? Buy a newer and bigger one, upgrade all your furniture, or relandscape the backyard—and while you're at it, invest in a hot tub. The fact is, the more HGTV you watch, the less satisfied you'll be with your home and/or garden.

The more scrolling you do on social media apps, the more you'll feel disenchanted with your clothes, your vacations, your neighborhood restaurants, even your dog.

It's easy to suggest unplugging and stepping away from it all—but in actuality, it can be rather challenging. That's okay. Go Slow and begin to notice when you are feeling anxious or disenchanted, and see if you can create a few screen-free breaks for yourself throughout the day.

Go outside and start being aware of your surroundings and becoming immensely grateful for all that you *do have* and *do get* to experience.

> "A calm and modest life brings more
> happiness than the pursuit of success
> combined with constant restlessness."
> —Albert Einstein

# What Is Slow Living?

I get asked to define Slow Living quite often through my work on the *Slow Living* podcast. The easiest way for me to sum it up in a neat and tidy sound bite is that Slow Living isn't a thing, it's a mindset. And the mindset is "faster and more does *not* equal better."

When you decide to Slow Down and not rush through life, even somewhat mundane tasks can take on a joyful and peaceful pleasure. It's actually easier for me to explain what Slow Living is *not* than what it is.

- Slow Living is not minimalism. But it can be.
- Slow Living is not deciding to only have a certain number of everyday items. But it can be.
- Slow Living is not selling your home, all of your possessions, and moving into a tiny house or an RV. But it can be.

Slow Living is a way to live life on your own terms. You can still have goals and aspirations, but you don't have to sacrifice your well-being or sanity (and that of your loved ones) to achieve them.

Slow Living is a lifestyle movement that emphasizes the importance of enjoying life's simple pleasures. It's about making deliberate choices and focusing on what truly matters, rather than rushing through life trying to do as much as possible in as little time as possible.

This often includes things like spending time in nature, being mindful and present in the moment, reducing stress, and simplifying life by decluttering and focusing on what is truly important. The goal of Slow Living is to cultivate a sense of balance, contentment, and well-being by living a more fulfilling and meaningful life.

I like this shortened definition:

*Slow Living is being consciously aware of what you are doing, what your surroundings are, and where you are headed in life.*

This means that you're actively living the life that you have consciously and purposefully *decided* on—one that is fulfilling, satisfying, and intentional. It also means that you trust that you can meet your personal and professional goals in a thoughtful, methodical, and sustainable way.

In a nutshell, Slow Living is not accidental living.

I have three children, and I currently work in an elementary school. I hear children bickering an awful lot—which means I hear the phrase, "But it was an accident!" more often than I can count.

And accidents? They usually aren't ever a good thing. That's why when cars bump each other, or when somebody falls off of a ladder, the term "accident" is used.

But *on purpose?* That's when you *consciously decide and plan* how things are going to happen. And that's what I'd like you to do in all aspects of your life.

Slow Living is also about being aware of your surroundings, of other people, and of what you are doing to the Earth and its future inhabitants. You're not alone on this planet, and you don't live in a vacuum. If you continue your current trajectory, what will your life look like in five years? In twenty years? Is what you are doing now meaningful and sustainable?

Some potential benefits of living a slower, calmer, and more peaceful lifestyle include:

1.  *Reduced stress and anxiety.* By intentionally slowing down and simplifying your life, you may

experience a greater sense of calm and reduced physical stress.

2.  *Improved mental health.* Slowing down can help you focus on what is truly important, leading to greater contentment, satisfaction, and overall mental well-being.

3.  *Increased mindfulness.* Living slowly encourages you to stay present and attentive to the moment at hand, which allows you to enhance your ability to enjoy simple pleasures and everyday experiences instead of dwelling on the past or worrying about the future.

4.  *Better relationships.* When you Slow Down and consciously decide to spend quality time with loved ones, your relationships improve and connections deepen.

5.  *Inspired creativity.* When you prioritize living a Slow Life, you may find that you have much more time and space for creative pursuits.

While the benefits of living a Slow Life on purpose can vary depending on individual circumstances, life experiences, and priorities, most people who decide to live this way report that they have a newfound sense of fulfillment, peace, and an overall feeling of well-being.

Some people embark upon their path to Slow Living because of an upheaval in their life: a medical diagnosis, a divorce, or a death in the family. My hope is that you are here out of curiosity, not because of tragedy, but no matter why you picked up this book, I'm glad you did.

## Warding Off Burnout

A little bit of stress can be beneficial—it keeps us alert, productive, and moving forward to our goals by helping us feel ambitious and motivated. However, too much stress can result in physical, emotional, and behavioral symptoms that may lead to serious illness or disease.

The following table lists some effects of stress and how they can manifest in your brain and body:

### Recognizing Symptoms of Stress

(This list is not exhaustive; not all symptoms are indicative of stress but are listed for awareness. Adapted from National Health Service UK.[3])

| Physical | Emotional/ Cognitive | Behavioral | Chronic |
|---|---|---|---|
| Asthma | Anger | Disrupted sleep, diet, and exercise | Anxiety disorders |
| Back pain | Brain fog | Conflict with others | Depression |
| Chest pain | Decreased libido | Nail biting | Heart disease |
| Fatigue | Inability to concentrate | Procrastination | Memory impairment |
| Headaches | Irritability | Racing thoughts | Poor diet & exercise habits |
| Indigestion | Mood instability | Restlessness | Skin diseases |

| Physical | Emotional/ Cognitive | Behavioral | Chronic |
|---|---|---|---|
| Migraines | Worry | Social withdrawal | Substance abuse |
| Nausea | | Substance abuse | Sleep disorders |
| Sweating | | Teeth grinding | Weakened immune system |

It's important to pay attention to these symptoms and markers of stress before they develop into something larger. I've seen far too often that if you don't decide to Slow Down, your body may eventually do it for you. And that's not fun.

## Slow Down to Have More

Throughout this book, we will work together to map your dream life that you will then decide to live on purpose.

We will do so with the help of tools I have developed over twenty years of studying self-help and personal development books, and through feedback from hundreds of thousands of people from all over the world who have visited my websites, read my books, and listened to my podcast episodes.

My goal for you is that by completing the exercises in this book, you'll be well on your way to living the life of your absolute dreams—a life where you feel as if you're thriving instead of merely surviving. Together, let's do this in a calm, sustainable, and immensely enjoyable way.

# Part 1

# Mindset:
# The Why

This first part of the book is designed to establish a clear definition of Slow Living—what it is, why it's so important to understand, how a slowdown mindset is connected to and affected by our feelings, and what it looks like to venture down a path of living not only more slowly but also more meaningfully and purposefully.

I'll introduce a tool I've developed to help you step out of a cycle of Automatic Negative Thoughts (ANTs) and "step into" thoughts that lead to greater opportunities to experience positive feelings that move you toward the life of peace, joy, and purpose you've longed to enjoy.

We will examine some of the roots of the pervasive Hustle Culture and explore the reasons its effects are so corrosive on our lives.

And we'll establish an important foundation for the rest of our time together using the illustration of the Peace Pyramid.

Are you ready? Buckle up and get ready to dream *big*. Let's get started!

# Chapter 1

# The First Step to Dreaming Big: Harmonizing Mind, Body, and Spirit

"Change your thinking, change your life."
—Ernest Holmes

My eldest daughter studied psychology for her undergrad degree and came home one day with a new-to-me acronym: ANT.

Automatic Negative Thoughts.

I immediately fell in love with this acronym and began using it with my coaching clients because the visual of ANTs is just so clear for so many of us.

Dr. Daniel Amen coined the term ANT in the early 1990s after he had a self-described hard day at the office and came home to a swarm of ants in his kitchen.[4]

When you first get ants in your kitchen (the insects, not the intrusive thoughts), you'll find that instead of thousands and thousands all coming into your home at once, the colony sends out one or two "scouter ants" to test the trail and see if it's safe.

If all is found to be okay, the scouter ants go back to the group with the message, and suddenly you're inundated with teeny-tiny bugs.

The key to preventing a massive influx is to snuff out these scouter ants as soon as you discover them (I'm sorry to all the bug lovers out there!) so they don't have the opportunity to go back and invite their friends.

This is a great metaphor for how to approach negative thoughts. If you find that you're having a recurring thought that isn't serving you, try to eliminate it as best you can before it multiplies and invites in other negative thoughts.

Here are a few examples of negative thoughts that don't serve you:

- *I'll never be able to afford a house.*
- *The economy is in ruins.*
- *Why would anyone want to hire me?*
- *I'm so ugly, there's no way that person would want to talk to me.*
- *What's the point of sending that email when they are going to say no anyhow?*

It's important to snuff out these unhelpful thoughts, or they will infiltrate your subconscious to the point that they become self-fulfilling prophecies. Motivating yourself to get going on a new project or idea is especially difficult if you're constantly beating yourself up in your brain.

With time and practice, you'll soon learn your own secret ANT-squashing formula. The best way that I have found to do this is to "pay myself first"—and I'm not talking primarily about money here. While financial advisors use this term to teach clients to automatically transfer from their paycheck into savings, the concept also applies to any of your own needs. When you pay yourself first, you're in a calmer and more stable position to help others. This usually comes in the form of journaling, meditation, yoga, a walk in nature, or taking a few deep breaths.

When you interrupt negative thoughts and focus on something new, you'll immediately begin to feel better, since thoughts usually come with accompanying feelings. And focusing on your feelings is the best way to bring about long-lasting, sustainable change for the better within your life because it's the easiest way to upgrade your mindset.

## Identifying Feelings

When you're trying to accomplish anything new or achieve a goal or personal milestone, you're doing so because you are certain that you'll feel better once you accomplish it.

If your goal is to lose weight or become more fit, the idea most people have is that the uncomfortable feeling they have by being overweight or out of shape will completely dissipate once the weight has shifted. Or perhaps your long-term goal is to get out of debt and reach financial independence. These are goals worth striving toward and achieving, but once you do reach the fitness or financial milestone, you can't tell yourself that you won't ever feel fear, worry, or doubt again. That's not how goal setting or living the life of your dreams should work.

UC Berkeley researchers identified twenty-seven distinct categories of emotion and published their findings in the *Proceedings of the National Academy of Sciences* journal in 2017.[5]

These findings were used to help update and create the emojis found in your computer and phone messaging software.

If you rank the emotions from highest and most positive to lowest and most negative, the chart may read something like this:

1. Bliss/Peace
2. Knowledge/Satisfaction
3. Passion
4. Enthusiasm
5. Eagerness
6. Optimism
7. Hopefulness
8. Neutral
9. Boredom
10. Pessimism
11. Irritation
12. Impatience
13. Overwhelmed
14. Disappointment
15. Doubt
16. Worry
17. Bewilderment
18. Blame
19. Discouragement
20. Anger
21. Revenge
22. Rage/Hate
23. Jealousy/Insecurity
24. Guilt
25. Unworthiness
26. Despair/Depression
27. Powerlessness

In schools and childcare centers, we use a similar list of feelings and emotions to help children visualize and understand better. The children can hold a little stuffed critter in their hands and use it to identify whatever feeling they are currently having.

Disney has used cartoon characters to explain emotions in the movie *Inside Out* (and its sequel). In this animated feature, the characters Joy, Sadness, Anger, Fear, and Disgust seemingly control the emotional reactions of eleven-year-old Riley as she and her family move from Minnesota to San Francisco.

The idea is to identify where you are, and then to refocus toward a more pleasing emotion. If you find that you hover around despair or discouragement, it might feel a bit better in your body if you decide to reach toward a feeling of hope or optimism.

The best way to mitigate these feelings is to try and shift to thoughts that will serve you, rather than deter you, since emotions often follow thoughts.

In the international bestselling book *Psycho-Cybernetics* by Maxwell Maltz, we learn that by changing our subconscious thoughts (also known as *automatic* thoughts) to those that will help move us toward our dreams and goals, not only can we achieve amazing and wondrous things, but we will feel good along the way.[6]

And isn't that what makes life fun and exciting? Enjoying the journey while we move our way through the unchartered territory of fulfilling our inner dreams, desires, and goals?

Let's go back to those twenty-seven feelings. When I first read through the list and had the idea to "reach for a better feeling thought," I envisioned a set of monkey bars on a playground. If you're clinging to a bar, you'll need to loosen your grip and reach for the next rung, or one close to it, in order to complete the set of monkey bars and get to the other side.

In real life, there really isn't "the other side" unless we're talking about death. And since we really don't know what death will feel like or be like, it's best to take note of all of these thoughts and feelings while we are still here on Earth and not try to rush through them.

If you try super hard to rush through feelings to get to the other side, you'll feel a bit frantic and as if you're behind. You also might feel like you're doing something wrong if you want to take your time. That frantic energy and discomfort is what Hustle Culture preys upon—and that's exactly what we are trying to counteract through living a Slow Life on purpose.

So instead of envisioning a linear set of monkey bars on a playground, try to envision a long and winding path through a rolling hillside filled with ups and downs and all-arounds. Real life is most certainly not linear, and on any given day you'll find yourself feeling the vast majority, if not all, of the feelings on the list. The secret is to pay attention to what you're feeling and not shove it away or dismiss it.

Back to the ANTs in the kitchen—the Automatic Negative Thoughts Dr. Amen identified that sometimes feel as if they are swarming all around our brains. If Dr. Amen and Dr. Maltz are right, and we can snuff out and reprogram negative thoughts into those that make us feel better and serve us, we can feel better right this second, in the present, not only when we hit whatever goal we are striving to reach.

Goals and dreams and wishes and wants are important to the human experience. But if feeling better all the time was the only thing to strive for, we'd all just reach for the quickest and easiest way to feel better—even if that thing isn't good for us, such as drugs or alcohol.

If we are lucky, life is long. Shortening life by chasing the fastest and quickest way to feel better is not something I, nor anyone else, would ever advocate. Instead, I'm proposing that we take our time on this journey through life and enjoy as much of it as possible.

And the very best way to do so . . . is to take it slow.

## Ask Good Questions, Get Good Answers

It's often said that the only stupid questions are the ones that don't get asked. So let's start asking *all* the questions.

Recall our acronym SLOW: Simply Look Only Within. Trust that Maxwell Maltz was correct and that your instincts are already programmed to help keep you safe and out of trouble and that if you take your time and ask open-ended questions, your brain will naturally supply an answer.[7]

When you Go Slow and ask yourself open-ended questions such as, *What is the best next step for me to take?* or *What is my body trying to tell me?* you'll find that your brain will respond with teeny voices that bubble up when you're trying to fall asleep, or in the shower, or while stuck in traffic. These little voices, whims, or nudges are sometimes called your intuition, inner guidance, the Universe, or the voice of God.

I'd like you to pay attention to these whims, nudges, and impulses because they are guiding you toward something, and that something is your destiny—these little voices should not be ignored. For example, they might whisper:

- Maybe it's time to stop smoking.
- It would feel better to be more active.
- Cutting down on drinking sounds wise.
- Stay away from creepy Jerry at work.
- Send the email today about that job posting.

All of these gentle tugs are signs and signals that you need to take action. If you've found that you've been ignoring these inner nudges or intuitive thoughts, please know that you're not alone and that it isn't your fault.

We were raised and conditioned from a very young age to quell our urges and impulses and follow the advice and wisdom of the adult experts in the room. Our first go-to experts were likely our parents, who told us when to eat and sleep, how to dress, and whether or not to trust certain groups of people. As we meandered our way through school, our teachers and professors filled us with the ideas and thoughts they believed we needed to navigate our way through life.

Once we hit adulthood, and our structured schooling was over, many of us had a difficult time shifting from the notion that someone, somewhere has all the answers and that if we would only keep researching and searching and striving, we could find this someone with the master answer key to pass the final test.

Spoiler alert: there isn't one fix-it-all expert solution. Even better news: I am giving you permission to stop searching and seeking—instead I am here to invite you to simply *Slow Down*.

Now let's begin the process of doing just that.

# Chapter 2

# Discover Your Mission: Your Slow Living Journey Begins

"When you discover your mission, you
will feel its demand. It will fill you with
enthusiasm and a burning desire
to get to work on it."
—W. Clement Stone

The answers you are chasing won't be found in a social media doomscroll or by watching another online video. The answers to your big questions about how to live the life of your dreams will come from within. As you read this book and work through the included exercises, I will help you relearn to listen to and trust your inner voice and intuition.

Our tools will include the 5 Steps to Slow Living and the concept of the Peace Pyramid. That's right: there are only five steps needed to live a Slow Life. I will explain them fully in Part 2, but here is a quick overview:

| 5 Steps to Living a Slow Life |
| --- |
| 1. Declutter Everything (use the PROM method) |
| 2. Know Where You Are Headed (set your GPS) |
| 3. Surround Yourself with Positivity / Stay in a Grateful State |
| 4. Take Action Daily (baby steps and ten-minute chunks) |
| 5. Tweak and Fine-Tune as Needed |

Before we delve into the steps, let's lay a sturdy foundation. In my Simple Shortcuts to Peace online course, I teach the concept of the Peace Pyramid. As we learned in grammar school, a pyramid is the most stable and solid of all man-made structures.

There are six components of the Peace Pyramid, and this is how we are going to design the life of your dreams.

The bottom level consists of *Time Management*, *Health*, and *Finances*. Once that's stable we move up a level to *Organization* and *Relationships*. When these five components are set and steady, we can add the top piece to our pyramid, which is *Peace*.

| Peace |
| --- |

| Organization | Relationships |
| --- | --- |

| Time Management | Health | Finances |
| --- | --- | --- |

The reason I teach goal setting and achieving this way is because, in general, most people are chasing an elusive feeling of well-being and happiness—or Peace.

Many times people think that they'll feel better, happier, or more at peace if they meet a certain financial goal or finally achieve six-pack abs. But what's the point of chasing only one component in life if you neglect the others?

I'm sure we've all heard stories of the daring entrepreneur who built a thriving business only to have her family pack up and move out while she was on a business trip. Or perhaps you've heard about the die-hard romantic couple who put their date nights and repeat honeymoons above all else and ended up needing to file for bankruptcy. Maybe you've secretly wished that your home was as clean and organized as the home of a woman in your Bible study, only to learn later that when visitors left she yelled at her children and they couldn't wait to grow up and move far away.

Peace, happiness, fulfillment, and a sense of overall well-being come from knowing deep down inside that you are meeting all of your personal and professional goals without neglecting any of the components of a life well-lived.

I'm not sure about you, but I hate being told what to do. I don't even like it when the person telling me what to do is *me*. That said, you picked up this book for a reason, and my hunch is that you feel, deep down inside, that there must be an easier way to live your life than feeling as if you're "behind" or that it doesn't matter what you do—it's never going to be good enough.

I'm so happy you're here.

## The Big Question Is *How?*

Together, we are going to map out a pyramid.

Long-term, stable, and reliable success means that *all* areas of your life are working in a cohesive manner.

I don't want you to focus only on one area of your life and let the others fall by the wayside. Rewriting your life through Slow Living means taking a comprehensive approach to success.

When my children were young, we spent a lot of time cuddled on the couch watching *Dora the Explorer*. Dora was certain that we could get *anywhere* if only we took the time to consult the map and take the course that made the most sense and had the least amount of obstacles.

Now, there *will* be obstacles. That's just how life is. And everybody has different obstacles. But when you Go Slow, ask yourself good questions, and let the answers come to you rather than trying to follow a path defined or dictated by others, you'll always have better results.

If all of us could just follow a set recipe and get the same result, the world would be filled with cookie-cutter success stories. We were all handed a different game board with different pieces and a different set of rules. You'll have the best success when you learn how to play your own particular game in the best way that serves you.

But the game is not Chutes and Ladders. You won't fall down a slide and go back to square one if you take a while to figure out your own personal game board. It's okay if you let your foot off of the gas just for a bit to properly chart your course.

Where are we headed? To the top of the pyramid—to Peace!

When these components are in place, you can finally feel as if there is enough time for the want-tos in life that you keep putting off.

The bottom layer of the pyramid is composed of *Time Management*, *Health*, and *Finances*, with the next level being *Relationships* and *Organization*.

All of these components need to be "in check" in order for you to feel at peace.

If you are struggling with any of these sections, it will be difficult to achieve the calm, cool, collected, and at-peace feeling you're after. The good news is that you really *can* take care of all of these have-tos—and it's not as complicated as you might imagine.

With that in mind, let's go back to our 5 Steps to Slow Living cheat sheet and apply each step within our Peace Pyramid.

## Planning Out Your Dream Life

It may sound quite type A and over-the-top controlling, but the best way to Slow Down your life is to actually plan it out.

What I mean by that may be different from exercises you've done in the past, because while I will help guide you through the components of the Peace Pyramid—where you're ultimately headed—*how* you input the coordinates of your GPS (global positioning system) will be completely up to you.

This is important, because if you're living a life defined by someone else's terms, or by following the "rules" somebody else has created—society, your parents, your spouse, religious teachings, etc.—you will not feel fulfilled, even if you "check off all the boxes" according to that plan.

I'd like you to take some time here and try to envision where you'd like to go.

- If you are a student in school, fast-forward and think about where you see yourself in five years or so, after you graduate.
- If you are a newlywed, fast-forward five to ten years and really take the time to "see" in your daydreams

what your life looks like, in each of the components of the Peace Pyramid.

- If you are in the midst of parenting, what does it look like when the children leave the nest?
- How will your retirement years look?

Keep the following questions in mind as you map out your vision for your future self:

- What does your day-to-day routine look like? (Time Management)
- What does your health look like, whether physical, mental, or emotional? (Health)
- How much money do you have in the bank? What income are you producing? (Finances)
- What does your home environment look like, and what material items do you possess? (Organization)
- Who are the dominant players in your life, and how do you feel about them? (Relationships)
- How do you feel on a daily (or almost daily) basis? (Peace)

In order to dream or envision the future, some of you may need to suspend your disbelief for a while, or at least put it on the shelf. For others, this will come quite naturally because you already tend to be a dreamer or have an active imagination.

As for me, I'm quite the dreamer and have always had a very active imagination. I don't necessarily need to see the "hows" in order to believe that what I'm dreaming about can come true.

My husband, on the other hand, is an engineer and has a hard time imagining things without seeing an exact clear path to getting there.

It's up to you how you allow yourself to get to this place of suspending your disbelief. Many people lean on their own practiced religion or organized faith as a bit of a shortcut, but as far as I'm concerned, there is no right or wrong way.

You get to decide what works for you and your own particular life.

**"To thine own self be true."**
**—Shakespeare**

## How Woo Are You?

I grew up Presbyterian. I went to Sunday school, attended Vacation Bible Camp during the summer, went to sleepaway church camp in middle school, and hung out in the teen room for youth group.

I have read the Bible front to back, can quote a few verses, recite prayers, and sing along to hymns.

But I grew up in the San Francisco Bay Area and still live here now. This means that some of my closest friends were (and still are) atheists. I taught preschool for a while at a Jewish Temple, and I know an awful lot of facts about the High Holy Days.

I married into a Catholic family, and each morning I walk Sheldon, the family basset hound, past the local Catholic church and say a silent prayer of thanks and gratitude to the statue of Mary.

I also read my horoscope daily, flip over oracle cards, burn sage to cleanse evil spirits, rearrange furniture to keep the chi in check, and regularly pray, meditate, do yoga, and chant affirmations. I haven't quite gotten into crystals, but a friend is eager to teach me all about them when I'm ready.

When pressed about my beliefs, I merely state that I believe in the things that serve me, and let the other stuff go.

The nice thing about belief and faith is that you don't have to understand all of the minute details of the How and the Why—you can just accept that somehow, somewhere, it's all working.

For those of you who aren't eager to place any faith outside of the human condition, I say this: We all get a little bit religious or spiritual each time we step onto an airplane or are sitting in a hospital waiting room while a loved one is undergoing surgery. Tap into that feeling.

## Is It Real or a Placebo?

The weird thing about faith is that once you have decided to believe in it, you begin to see examples of it working all around you.

Science calls this cognitive bias.

Skeptics call it coincidence.

Some people call it the Law of Attraction.

I call it carefully planning and mapping out the life of your dreams. Before you dismiss me as spouting off a whole mess of mumbo jumbo, stop and think about it. The most well-researched and famous cognitive bias of them all is the placebo effect.

If you or a loved one were in a drug trial because of a debilitating disease, and the pills given worked to reverse the disease, would you care if the "medicine" was real or a sugar pill? No. If the disease was knocked out, it was knocked out.

The end result is all that matters.

## But What About Bad Things?

Religious scholars and disciples of all faiths ponder this question incessantly: If you have faith, why do bad things continue to happen?

If you believe hard enough, won't God or the Universe protect you from bad things? Did evil thoughts bring about sickness, famine, drive-by shootings, or a devastating flood?

The simple answer is no. The more complex answer is that humans like to know all of the answers, and sometimes we simply don't have an acceptable explanation for how and why things occur. My best suggestion for you is to let thoughts and worries go that aren't helpful to your growth and development.

## Why Are We Racing, Anyway?

When my family first moved into our current neighborhood, an older lady who lived up the street would come out each morning in her robe, slippers, and some sort of shower cap to yell at the speeding cars.

I am not being insulting by describing her as a little old lady. She was in fact old. And appeared to be quite small in size. Anyhow, this street is busy—it leads straight to the freeway on-ramps for either San Francisco or San Jose.

I'm sure you can imagine that during certain hours, drivers are speeding—either up the hill to get to the freeway for work, or back down the hill to get home after a long day.

This lady would come out with a homemade picket sign and shake it at the cars. In thick, dark-reddish Magic Marker it read . . .

## SLOW THE %#&* DOWN

. . . except that it didn't say %#&*. Instead, it read the actual word that I'm sure your brain can figure out.

She was awesome.

The sign was awesome.

And the sentiment?

*TOTALLY AWESOME!*

Whenever I find myself feeling a bit frantic or frenzied, I think about that lady. She has since passed away, but I can see her clearly in my mind, and I use this memory as a reminder that it's okay to Go Slow.

Faster does not mean better. I'm still going to get where I want to go.

## Chasing Likes, Grades, and Gold Stars

If you were raised in a somewhat Westernized world, you were taught at a very (very!) early age to live on someone else's terms and adhere to someone else's agenda. This began right from day one when you needed to garner another human's attention to feed you, rock you, change you, and comfort you.

That's not your fault, nor the fault of your parents—it's just what it is.

A bit later, though, most of us were raised to be sort of glorified "trained seals"—performing to please our parents, then teachers, then bosses at work. For many of us, this continues well into our adult lives, performing for "likes" and "shares" on social media channels, or trying our hardest to impress our neighbors and acquaintances.

But because of this, you may not be living a life that you like, much less one that you designed on purpose. Again, this is no one's fault.

That said, the sooner you figure out what you'd like your life to look like, and how you will fill your days, the happier and more fulfilled you will feel.

This happens naturally in the human experience. Unfortunately for many of us, it occurs after a debilitating diagnosis or a traumatic event that shakes us enough to reexamine our lives. We then start to incorporate new ways of living and habits that we think will take us where we want to go or where we think that we *should* go.

Now let's pause here for a bit and Slow Down. Think about this loaded word—*should*—and its frequent counterpart, *shame*. Brené Brown writes in her powerful book *The Gifts of Imperfection* that shame is the fear of social disconnection.[8]

Since humans are dependent on others for survival, we are deemed social animals—different from a sea turtle, for instance, who is truly on his or her own after emerging from the shell.

The need for human-to-human connection and approval from others (parents, teachers, coworkers, friends, online acquaintances) is so strong that going against the "norm" or paving our own way in life is often truly painful.

Neuroscience has shown that being disconnected, shunned, or kicked out of the pack registers as actual pain in our brain receptors. This is relevant because in order to help alleviate these painful feelings, we tend to settle for doing what others expect of us—even if it means we dismiss our own thoughts, ideas, and feelings.

So we do the things in life that we think we *should*. Even when we don't want to.

And a lot of this has to do with the original acronym for FOMO and with the Joneses.

FOMO (fear of missing out) is an acronym that, according to *Boston Magazine*, got its origin in the early 2000s.[9] It became prevalent in our everyday vernacular in about 2010, when social media and texting became entrenched into all aspects of life.

Missing out is a very real fear for humans because the idea that the rest of our tribe, the rest of our counterparts, are off doing activities or having fun and experiences *without us* leaves us feeling unloved, unworthy, unchosen, and vulnerable. This feeling evokes shame.

It's tricky, because in order to find true friends who are grounded and have qualities you admire and want to emulate, you need to deeply and truly know yourself first.

And to do that, it's time for us to rewrite FOMO, once and for all. For the purposes of our journey together, I invite you to think of the acronym as:

**F**igure
**O**nly
**M**yself
**O**ut

This is the missing piece. That is your life's work. You need to figure out what *you* actually *want* and what you're working toward.

When you're younger, you follow checklists and guidelines that somebody else created. At some point, you need to become fully in charge of your life and where you are going, otherwise you'll end up feeling restless and unfulfilled.

The more you focus on FOMO as defined above, the greater chance you'll have to dream of a more fulfilling, peace-filled life—and don't you think it's high time to let those kinds of dreams take shape?

# Chapter 3

# The Real FOMO: Why Meeting All Your Goals Won't Give You Purpose

"Dreaming, after all, is a
form of planning."
—Gloria Steinem

One of the best ways to begin your Slow Living path is to give yourself permission to "zone out" or daydream.

I've always been a dreamer. Some of my earliest memories from elementary school are hearing the teacher—from what sounded like a great distance—calling out my name.

"Steffie? Steffie, are you with us? Steffie, can you hear me?"

I would startle and see that Mrs. Greigh was leaning directly over me, frantically waggling her fingers toward my face, trying to "snap me" out of whatever trancelike state I appeared to be in.

I liked my dreams. They were fun and cozy and safe and lovely—my own comforting place I could retreat to and revisit whenever I felt unsure or anxious.

I was in second grade when I realized that if I tried hard enough, I could make my daydreams come true. Yes, long before *The Secret* hit the mass market or I took a psychology class that taught me how to harness the power of my subconscious mind, I was turning my dreams into reality.

It started with Whiskers, my hamster.

I'm not certain the exact bargaining or creatively persuasive words I used to convince my parents that at age seven I was responsible enough to be a hamster parent—but I do remember the day that my mom and dad told me, over dinner on a Friday night, that after I cleaned up, we would head to the pet store in the mall to pick out a hamster of my very own.

As I brushed my teeth, I began crying, which alarmed my dad. He stood in the doorway of the bathroom with a very puzzled look on his face.

"Steffie? Are you okay?"

I answered through my sobbing tears, intermingled with toothpaste foam, "Oh, yes! I'm just so very happy!"

Looking back at that day, now as an adult in my mid-forties, this was a pivotal milestone in my growth and development. It was the first example I can remember of how I discovered that if I wanted something badly enough, I could find a way to make it happen.

The examples of my puppet mastery turned into reality continued to add up as I navigated my teen and college years, and still to this day, I have found a way to make many of the things that I daydreamed about come true.

I dreamt of having a best friend.

I daydreamed of getting a puppy.

I hoped and wished and prayed for a boyfriend who would love me for exactly who I was and that we would live a long, healthy, and happy life together with three children. My husband, Adam, and I met when we were both sixteen and have now been very happily married for over two decades.

I agonized over how to pay off our consumer debt so we could start shoveling money into bank accounts.

I daydreamed about quitting my job to stay home with my kids.

I dreamt of speaking on stage.

I daydreamed about someday being a best-selling author and appearing on national television.

I dreamt about what kind of house I'd have, complete with white cabinets and gray kitchen countertops, that I'd drive a minivan, and how I'd have the lushest front yard of anyone on our block.

Big things and little things—it really didn't matter to me what I dreamt or how far-fetched my thoughts seemed to others. I just kept dreaming.

And so far, many of the things I've dreamt about have found a way to come true.

Having said that, let me add that life is not always perfect. We know that not every dream comes true. Some are deferred; others shift and morph over time. And remember: *This is not a race, and you aren't in a competition with anyone. This is your life, and if you are lucky, it'll be filled with lots of experience and adventure.*

So Go Slow, and enjoy the journey.

## Planning the Dream

I've always been a planner and have liked checking things off of to-do lists. When I was a newlywed and young mother, I loved listening to books on tape and learning about all things having to do with personal development. I enjoyed reading success stories about self-made millionaires and tried my hardest to create systems and routines for every aspect of my life.

These routines helped create the scaffolding I needed to keep moving forward on the trajectory I wanted.

It helped that I have always worked with young children and saw firsthand that routines and schedules were helpful to keep the day running smoothly and the better planned the day was, the better behaved the children were.

I still try to plan my days, although I now incorporate long stretches of time that are blocked off that merely say "thinking and writing time," and I also schedule in walks and naps. Planning ahead to actively be slow is one of the best tools and suggestions I can offer you.

## What Does the Future Look Like?

When I was in my late twenties, I was close friends with a group of moms online. We chatted multiple times a day on a message board and had long-written discussions about our family life, what we wanted for our futures, and how to best plan out our days with small children in the home. We also shared recipes and cleaning tips.

One of the exercises we did to get to know one another and to help envision our future was to write our obituaries. I was pretty young at the time and didn't really want to fast-forward all the way to my late eighties or early nineties.

But I did make a list of things that I wanted to do, and be known for.

So what about you? If you were to take the time to write your obituary right now, what would it say? What would you *want* it to say, and how can you go about changing the trajectory you're currently on in order to have these things come to fruition?

If writing an obituary seems a bit morbid and not something you're comfortable with, how about a letter from the future? This is something that I have done multiple times, and something that I ask my life coaching clients to do.

You don't need to share this letter with anyone, but I'd like you to read your letter at least once a week. This is a simple exercise, but it will really help you in the upcoming chapters when we work together to map out the life that you want to live slowly and on purpose.

Take out a piece of paper or open a new document. Date it ten years from now and start writing.

*Dear* _____, *these past ten years have been the*
_____ *ever.*

*We have accomplished so many things, including:*
_____.

Ten years from now . . .

- What time do you wake up in the morning? Go to bed?
- How do you spend the majority of your time?
- What does your health look like? What do you weigh? What is your fitness level?
- How much money is in your savings account? Your investment accounts? Do you have consumer debt?

- Where are you living? What does the interior of your home look like? What kind of clothes do you wear?
- Who are the five people you spend the most time with, and what do they mean to you?

I read somewhere in one of the many time management books I've picked up over the years that millionaires review their goals once a day, and billionaires review their goals twice a day. I don't personally know any billionaires, but I do know plenty of millionaires, and all of them do take the time to plan out their futures.

Ironically, you might think that while I was writing cookbooks and speaking on stages that I *was* living out the life of my dreams. And I was, to a certain extent. I always knew that I wanted to write and to teach. But I thought it would be about goal setting or personal development.

The first time I appeared on national television was on *Rachael Ray*.[10] I was certain that after this appearance I'd be asked to write a memoir or a how-to book on fulfilling my New Year's resolution.

When book publishers began emailing me and asked me to write a cookbook, I initially balked. I was not a chef or a foodie—I was simply a mom who had an idea and decided to follow it through.

I cooked each night not because it was my passion, but because I had little kids in the house who needed to eat healthy, wholesome food.

> "I don't care what you do for a living.
> I want to know what you ache for and if
> you dare to dream for your life's yearning."
> —Oriah Mountain Dreamer

# Living in FOMO (Figure Only Myself Out)

Sometimes well-meaning adults tell us when we are growing up to "follow your passion" and trust that the money will follow. This is outdated advice for today's day and age.

While it may sound good and look great on a bumper sticker, it isn't practical to hope and blindly trust that you'll find a way to adequately fund your life with your passions and hobbies. Your job is merely how you make money. It does not need to equate to your life's purpose.

For a select few, their passion *is* the way that they bring money into their lives, but for the vast majority of us, this is not the case.

That's okay.

My current passions happen to include long naps, perfecting Warrior 3 in yoga, and going on beach walks with Sheldon, my basset hound.

I don't make money from my passions.

And I'm fine with that.

Wayne Dyer used to caution his readers and those who called in to his radio program by saying, "Don't die with your music still in you."[11] I wholeheartedly agree with this statement. But you don't need to make a living or provide for your family with this music. You can find a way to incorporate the things you *want* to do alongside the things you *need* to do.

And for most of us, we need to work and make money.

Making money and following your passion are *not* the same thing.

Please don't confuse the two.

# What Do You Want to Be
# When You Grow Up?

There's a funny internet meme in which adults keep asking children, "What do you want to be when you grow up?" because the grown-ups are still looking for ideas.

I'd like you to treat your job and your profession as something separate from your passion. I first got this idea when I read the book *Rich Dad, Poor Dad* by Robert Kiyosaki. He wrote that while his "poor dad" taught at the local university and thought of his job as his life's work, his "rich dad" looked at jobs as ways to provide money to do the things he wanted to do in life. He then used that money to invest in real estate, which is what excited him.

What if you released yourself from the pressure that tells you to find a way to make money from your passion?

When working with teens and young adults, I advise them to work backward when trying to figure out what they want to do as a career or major in at college. These are the questions I ask:

- Where do you want to live?
- What type of home will you have?
- Will you have a car? How much will this cost?
- Will you learn to cook and make most of your meals at home, or will you mostly eat out and/or order in?
- How much money will you need to make in order to maintain this lifestyle?

After coming up with a tentative lifestyle cost, we start looking for jobs that have a comparable salary, and then from there, they decide what type of schooling is necessary.

This is an important shift in the thought process of "following your passion" because it keeps the end goal in sight. If you want to live in Manhattan, you'll need to create a different reality for yourself than if you want to live in a midwestern suburb.

And the fact is, different people want different things in life.

I remember being at a writing and blogging conference where a presenter was talking about creating a "private jet" lifestyle. That idea seemed so foreign to me because I, personally, had no interest in ever flying on a super-small plane.

When my husband, Adam, and I were newlyweds, we took a flight over San Francisco with our friend Steve, who was training to be a pilot, in a four-seater plane named "The Duchess."

While circling over Candlestick Park (former home of the 49ers and Giants, now a condo development), the plane's side door suddenly swung open. Adam and I were in the back seat with only a lap belt on, and the door was *wide open*. Steve, cool as a cucumber, merely pulled the door back down, muttered, "Oh yeah, this happens sometimes with The Duchess," and held the door in place while he piloted the plane back down to the airstrip with one hand.

We were absolutely fine, but this experience has gotten "flying private" out of my system!

What about you? If you want to create a lifestyle in which you only fly private, you can. But please remember that you can absolutely feel fulfilled and content in your everyday life, regardless of how you travel.

## Identifying Your Personal Purpose

Chelsea, a listener of the *Slow Living* podcast, called in and asked how to go about finding your purpose.[12] She reported that after being a wife and mom for so many years, she didn't know anymore who she was and wasn't sure how to create goals for herself.

Within this episode, we explored the idea of going on a Vision Quest—taking the time to just sit in nature and let her mind wander freely. I've heard it said that everybody should sit in nature for at least twenty minutes a day, unless you're busy. Busy people should sit in nature for at least *an hour* a day.

We also talked about Chelsea perhaps creating a Vision Board—taking photos and words from magazines that she thought depicted items that represented her or things she'd like for her future, along with places and scenery that spoke to her.

A "Purpose" isn't a destination, however. Having purpose means that when you get out of bed in the morning, you're excited to see how the day unfolds because you are doing something you're interested in, or something that somehow feeds your soul.

But chasing one certain thing, one certain goal, and calling that a purpose won't ever feel gratifying or fulfilling—because when you've got blinders on and are simply chasing the goal, you'll feel a bit let down once you achieve it.

This happens often to brides on their wedding day: when they have spent years and years planning the perfect day, and it occurs exactly as they'd imagined, somehow they feel let down because they thought they'd somehow feel different or life would be different once that day happened.

This can also happen when you're in the process of losing weight and you entertain the thought that when you hit $X$ pounds, you'll finally be happy. Or when you land a certain promotion at work, or hit a particular number in your bank account.

Meeting all your goals won't give you purpose.

The stuff that happens along the way is what life is all about.

Life is a magical patchwork quilt of interests and hobbies and memories and relationships along with triumphs and failures.

These are the ingredients needed to make life interesting and fun to live. Have fun. Try things and be bold, but don't believe that your happiness is waiting for you on the other side of a certain goal or milestone.

It's here and it's now. Soak it in.

The same way I'd like you to release the notion that you should make money from your passion, I'd like you to release the idea that you were "put on this earth for a reason" and that there is only one true purpose for you and every other person.

There's not. You can have many different purposes in life and they can ebb and flow as you live your life.

Remember, if we are lucky, life is long. Who you are at age twenty-five is not who you are at age fifty-five or seventy-five—so explore.

Take new classes and follow interests that excite you. The Disney movie *Soul* is an excellent example of this. The main character spends the whole movie certain that he needs to live out his life's purpose, only to realize that along the way he has entertained many different aspects and interests that have given his life a ton of purpose and meaning.

When I was a young wife and mother, my big purpose was trying to find a way to be a stay-at-home mom. That was my dream, and it ended up materializing thanks to my slow-cooker adventures.

My purposes have changed here and there throughout the years, but the steadfast conviction I've always had—to be as present as I can in my children's lives and put my family before all else—has remained true.

Different passions have also bubbled up through the years—I wanted to learn how to write and speak on stage, and I got interested in yoga and running. For a while, my biggest project was crate-training Sheldon, the basset hound.

## Separating Your Job from Your Identity

Again, I don't want you to worry about monetizing your passion. You can separate who you are as a human from what you do to make a living.

You are not your profession. Many people use someone's job, or profession, as a shortcut to size them up and to decide how much respect they should bestow upon them.

It's rather gross.

Humans are all worthy of love, acceptance, and appreciation, regardless of what they choose to do (or not do) to make money.

My high school drama teacher gave us an exercise to practice our improvisation skills.

She handed a deck of cards to two people and asked them to take the stage. One student held the deck, with a card pointing out, against his or her forehead. The other student then began the scene talking as if the person were the exposed card—for instance, a two of spades was treated differently than the king of hearts, who was instantly revered and put on a pedestal.

I've personally witnessed and experienced this phenomenon multiple times in my adult life, and each time it happens it shakes me, but as the years pass, each circumstance rattles me less and less.

I first experienced it when I was about twenty-four years old at the grand opening of a childcare center built for homeless families. A reporter from the local newspaper who was there to cover the opening refused to make eye contact or speak with me until the main director of the large nonprofit agency confirmed that yes, I was in charge, and I was the right person to interview.

I chalked that experience up to ageism and just moved on.

Fast-forward eight to ten years and I was at a writing conference for food bloggers. My no-money-down blog had just been named the number three food blog in the US, and I was arriving to give a talk about monetizing your website.

I was worried beforehand about attending the conference because I don't consider myself a foodie; I just happened to be a food writer. That said, I was given a free pass to the conference and hotel accommodations because I was asked to be a speaker.

When I walked into the crowded ballroom for the pre-conference mixer wearing my name tag proudly, many of the writers I tried to engage in conversation made cordial small talk while looking over my head (not hard, since I'm only five feet tall!) so they could network with someone "better."

It wasn't until after I took the stage and the writers in the audience realized I was a "somebody" that they came up and played friendly and nice.

This feeling of not being good enough or feeling unworthy in group settings continued to come up through the years. I never knew how to answer the question, "What do you do?" Sometimes I answered I was a stay-at-home mom, sometimes a writer, and sometimes that I ran my own online business.

All of the answers were correct and accurate, but I was treated differently depending on the answer. In certain circles, if I answered I was a stay-at-home mom, I was dismissed. That feeling of being dismissed is awful, but it's just a feeling. Not a reality.

In order to continue writing and helping others, I have gotten used to this feeling and can now acknowledge it and move through the emotions without letting it hold me back. A big part of being a writer is rejection, and it's something that I have come to accept in order to make forward progress in my writing career.

Let's think about this for a bit and ponder how you interact with the people you meet in your life. Are you just as courteous to the busboy as you are to the hostess or restaurant manager? Do you think you're better than your Uber driver because you're the one sitting in the back seat?

My dad tells the story of traveling for business on a day when the airport terminal was especially busy and frenzied because of an air traffic delay. His arriving plane was running late. Frantic travelers, concerned about missing their connecting flight, crowded the desk where the lone service agent was feverishly trying to accommodate the growing line.

One man was noticeably upset and demanded that she "figure something out" for him. When she explained that her hands were tied, he yelled, "But don't you know who I am?!"

My dad says that she then grabbed the desk microphone, cleared her voice, and steadily stated into the microphone, "Excuse me, may I please have your attention? This gentleman is having a hard time knowing who he is. Is anyone able to assist him in figuring out who he is?" The man turned beet red and slunk off to sit, quietly, in the vinyl chairs of the waiting area.

I love this story because it illustrates that societal accolades, perceived prestige, and financial status really don't change who you are at your core.

If you act like a jerk, eventually it will catch up with you.

But what if you aren't a jerk, and you still can't seem to make strides toward what you seek in life?

When my husband and I first began dating, I remember feeling a bunch of self-doubt and insecurity about what I was going to be when I "grew up" and confided this in my new boyfriend. He hugged me tightly and muttered, "The root of all evil is low self-esteem."

I still think about that day and his words, now, thirty years later. I needed to have the strength and courage in myself to keep moving forward, and have faith in myself that when opportunities arose I would continue to do the next best thing.

That's what you need to do, too. In real life, you *do* need to find a way to live that provides enough of an income to support yourself and your family—even if your job isn't necessarily your deep-rooted passion.

It's okay to not monetize your passion.

Trust that you can live a very long, healthy, and satisfying life and that your "purpose" may change as you grow and evolve throughout your adult years. This is not only okay, but it's a great way to live.

I'm sure we've all come across the former high school football star who now, in his mid-fifties, is still telling the story of how he won the homecoming game at age sixteen.

In her memoir *Is Everyone Hanging Out Without Me?* actor Mindy Kaling writes that there is nothing more pathetic than someone bragging that they peaked in high school. She even picks apart the classic John Mellencamp song "Jack and Diane," in which he lyricizes that life goes on even after the thrills of those teenage years have passed us by. "Are you kidding me?" Kaling writes. "The thrill of living was high school? Come on, Mr. Cougar Mellencamp. Get a life."

No kidding! I don't know about you, but it helps me to remember that we haven't peaked yet and that many more thrills await. I hope one of them will greet you as we move into the *how* of the 5 Steps to Slow Living. Here we go!

# Part 2

# The Five Steps to Slow Living: The How

The second part of the Mindset + Action + Consistency = Success formula is Action. Many people jump to this section first because they are eager to find all the answers and have someone tell them what will be on the test.

There is no test.

This is your life, and you get to live it however you'd like. That said, within this second section I will teach you how to apply the 5 Steps to Slow Living to all aspects of your life as explained through the Peace Pyramid.

If you're looking for the "just tell me what to do, and then I'll do it!" portion of the book, this is it!

# Chapter 4

# Step 1: Declutter with the PROM Method

"Sometimes, when you are trying to
add to your life, the best thing you
can do is to start subtracting."
—Anonymous

If you want to figure out your purpose and have enlisted the help of a life coach, such as myself, to find it, what might that look like? Here's one story to give you an idea.

Jean Luc was in his early sixties when he and I worked together. His mom had passed away, he had just inherited her house, and he was processing his grief when we got on a coaching call. He was worried that his life hadn't "amounted to anything" because, although he had a doctorate in educational psychology, he'd spent the majority of his adult life caring for his mom and managing her life details.

Now that she was gone, there wasn't a pressing need to go to work because the estate provided plenty for his living expenses. I listened to him for close to an hour before I asked him if he had gone through the items left in his mom's home.

No, he confessed. He was continuing to live in his childhood bedroom and thought it would take close to a year to carefully and thoughtfully sort through the belongings.

Thinking about the 5 Steps to Slow Living, I gently encouraged him not to spend time worrying about his great big life purpose right now—but instead to simply start on Step 1 and declutter by utilizing the PROM method (discussed fully in the upcoming pages). I promised him that if he just had this as his day-to-day project and the reason to hop out of bed each morning, something "bigger" would come forth.

The same can be true for you as well, as we are about to discover together.

In Part 1, I introduced you to the acronym for living the life of your dreams on purpose—SLOW: Simply Look Only Within. In this section, we are going to lay out the game plan to make this way of living a reality and to bring your dreams to life.

And if you don't have a dream, that's okay. By taking the time to read this book and go through the exercises laid out within the 5 Steps to Slow Living and the Peace Pyramid, you'll end up with an idea and vision to work toward, I promise.

The first step to take if you're ready to Slow Down and live on purpose is to declutter. I'd like you to inventory all that you have in your life and begin to purge what is no longer serving you. Most people start with the physical things in their home, and that's a fantastic place to begin.

## Less Is More

As I stated earlier, I used to run preschool centers for disadvantaged children before I started a family of my own. Have you ever been inside a preschool or daycare center, or looked around a kindergarten classroom?

Every item has a home. Each shelving unit and bin is labeled, and every toy, art supply, and learning activity has a designated spot.

Because the center I managed happened to be within a homeless shelter, we were fortunate to receive a lot of donations. You'd think that the teachers, residents, and children would be overjoyed to receive carload after carload filled with toys, books, and puzzles.

And sometimes we were: clothing, food, and consumable items like toothpaste, bubble bath, and fancy-smelling shampoo were incredibly well-received, but after a while, the excess toys, books, and games were simply tossed.

It became too much to store, and we found that after a while, the children refused to even look up from what they were working on to paw through a cardboard box full of "new" things. They much preferred to pick from the carefully curated shelves with only a few items to choose from. It was also much easier to clean up before lunch and nap time!

In fact, all I needed to do was to set a timer for a 10-Minute Tidy (more on that concept later!), and the classroom was whipped into shape before the beeper sounded.

It may sound silly, but adults are an awful lot like preschoolers.

Think about how hotel rooms are laid out and decorated, or how a model home feels when you first walk in. The tabletops and countertops are cleared off, and there is ample open space.

When you have fewer items to store, it's much easier to keep everything neat and tidy.

I've got to admit here that while I *like* things neat and orderly, I don't actually *enjoy* the act of cleaning. In fact, if the lifestyle depicted on the futuristic animated series *The Jetsons* ever became the norm, I'd be first in line for a self-cleaning house filled with helpers like Rosie the Robot.

Since such a house hasn't been invented yet (although I do really love my Roomba!), I choose to do a little bit each day so the house isn't ever more than thirty minutes or so away from being able to entertain company.

If you find that you have too many personal items to store in a neat and tidy way, the first thing I recommend is to start decluttering.

An easy-to-remember acronym to help with this process is PROM. Don't worry, I'm not suggesting that you don a strapless turquoise gown covered in sequins. Today's PROM is not an overpriced school dance but an acronym for an efficient way to declutter.

If you're wondering right about now, *Hey, does Steph like acronyms or* what? the answer is yes. She really, really does!

## Let's Go to the PROM—Purge, Remove, Organize, Maintain

### P—Purge

Grab a garbage can or large plastic sack and get moving. When faced with a decluttering challenge, enter a room and quickly toss all items that are obviously garbage. Move as fast as you can and try not to overthink your decisions.

One Barbie shoe? Toss it.

Last year's invite to your third cousin's fourth son's baptism party that you didn't go to but the picture on the card reminds you of when your now-nine-year-old used to listen? Toss it.

Once you have filled your bin or your sack, put the lid on it or tie it up.

If your blood pressure has risen while reading the last few paragraphs, please take a slow, deep breath. I know this concept might feel really difficult, especially if you've ever lived in a state of lack or if you easily form emotional attachments to items, but I promise you there is so much reward on the other side of intentionally purging what isn't bringing you joy. Please stay with me!

The next pass through the room (or drawer, box, bookshelf—whatever it is you're purging) might not be so quick. With another bin or trash bag, assess the remaining items. Try to keep this simple:

- If you don't need it, toss it.
- If you can't remember what it is, toss it.
- If you don't know the last time you used it, but you think you might need it someday but you don't know when that will be, toss it.

Release the clutter and reclaim your home. The less "stuff" you have, the less you have to clean.

## R—Remove

This is partly a continuation of what we just covered. Get rid of your purged things quickly. Don't take a second look at them, and most certainly, don't let the bags of purged items sit around in a closet or garage long enough for children to rifle through them and discover lost treasure!

Take the garbage to the outdoor can or to the local dump right away.

Donate still-useful items to charity. There are numerous nonprofits listed online in your local area which would greatly benefit from your castoffs. Many will come to your home for a pickup, and they all offer tax-deduction receipts.

If you and your family would rather hold a garage sale, schedule it as soon as possible. Holding on to a pile of purged stuff to sell is almost as bad as if you never purged in the first place. Sell quickly and arrange for a charity drop-off or pickup to dispense with all remaining items.

## O—Organize

Take the time to organize the remaining items in your newly decluttered space. And let's keep it simple. Put like items together and use baskets or plastic bins to contain small items. Storage containers don't need to be expensive.

In our house, many of the bins we use to store toys, games, or clothing accessories came from the dollar store or are repurposed from other containers. Depending on space, consider installing extra shelves, hooks, or a pegboard to help maintain order.

If you find that you continue to have more items than available storage space, purge again with a more discerning eye.

Again, I know it's tough to get rid of things, but remember that it's the *people* in your house that count, not the *stuff*.

## M—Maintain

You've done all this work. Now it's time to make sure things don't spiral out of control again. Spend a little time daily putting things back where they belong. Take a photo of your hard work and hang it in the newly decluttered environment to remind children (and spouses!) what the space *should* and *can* look like with just a touch of effort. Create easy routines to help you consistently maintain this beautiful space you've created (more on this in Part 3).

Explain that it's everyone's responsibility, not just yours, to help ensure cleanliness and order.

Now, give yourself a pat on the back. Your children deserve to live in a decluttered, calm, and peaceful home. You deserve it, too.

As you continue working on the PROM method throughout your home, you'll be able to confidently say that you have a place for all of the items you bring into your living space. For some, this may take some doing, but I promise you'll feel calmer, less anxious, and more at peace when you take the time to purge, remove, organize, and maintain your personal items.

* * *

Heather, one of the students in my Simple Shortcuts to Peace course, recently spent time going through the items she inherited after her mom's passing last summer. This is the feedback she shared after taking a few months to thoughtfully purge:

"It was (is!) hard to part with a lot of things, but today, having less 'stuff' also means less apprehension. Less avoidance. Less anxiety. Less exclusion. Less loneliness. Less regret. Less shame. Today, less 'stuff' means more time. More hospitality. More relationships. More openness. More laughter. More gratitude. More joy. More LIFE!!"

## PROMing the Other Parts of Your Life

Earlier I explained the concept of the Peace Pyramid with five sections that connect to create a solid foundation for your life. As a reminder, the components of the Peace Pyramid are Time Management, Health, Finances, Organization, and Relationships.

Attention needs to be paid to each of these sections as you work through your PROMing.

Granted, purging and tossing excess *physical* clutter in your home is much easier than purging and tossing the intrusive thoughts, feelings, habits, emotions, and mental fatigue you may be experiencing, brought on by some of the behaviors, people, routines, and activities in your life.

Take some time here for a few minutes and think about your day-to-day routines. Are they helping you move toward your end goal?

- Is there something you can omit from your daily schedule or a different way to prioritize your time?
- What about your health? Are there any habits or lifestyle choices that aren't meeting your future goals that you can kick to the curb?
- How are your finances? Is there a recurring charge or bill that you can declutter?
- How organized would you say you are overall? Do you feel as if you have a good handle on the structure and direction of your life?
- And what about your relationships? Are your interactions with others helping or hindering you as you move toward your dream?

I'm not suggesting that you immediately disassociate from people in your life who don't consistently bring a feeling of joy, purpose, and serenity everywhere they go.

This is real life. And in real life, there are others who may or may not be on the same wavelength as you and who may be carrying around a lot of their own pain and trauma.

Let other people be other people, for now.

Later in the book, we will discuss how to carefully insulate yourself from people and daily events/activities (such as going to work or school) that may not "spark joy"— to borrow Marie Kondo's famous phrase.[13] For now, just keep reading, and feel content with the idea that you are in the beginning stages of creating the rest of your life.

## Less Decisioning

I've decided that *decisioning* is a word. Let's go with it. Decision fatigue is a real thing.

One of the amazing benefits of taking the time to declutter your home and life is that you end up with *more* time to do what you really want to do because you're no longer trying to please others or do what you think you "should" do.

I first realized I had a massive case of decision fatigue when I was a newish mother of an infant and a toddler who needed to eat real food that was healthy and accessible, multiple times a day.

After I looked in all the nooks and crannies of our suburban tract home for someone to "save me" (Prince Charming, a knight in shining armor, a fairy godmother, Martha Stewart, Mr. Belvedere . . .), I came to the painful conclusion that *I* was actually The Adult in Charge, and *I* needed to find a way to feed all of the beings in the house.

(This is originally why I fell in love with my slow cooker, which led to the AYearofSlowCooking.com website and subsequent books.)

So I created a meal plan.

And then I created a schedule.

Let's go back to the preschool classroom. One prominent feature in all classrooms filled with young children is the daily schedule.

It usually looks something like this:

| Opening Circle |
| --- |
| Math |
| Language |
| Recess |
| Art |
| Reading |
| Free Play |
| Lunch |
| Recess |
| Nap Time |
| Cleanup |
| Snack |
| Recess |
| Closing Circle |
| Pickup |

Having a schedule and a game plan means less decisioning. Another term for this is time blocking. A "Grown-Up" schedule may look something like this:

| |
|---|
| Wake Up |
| Morning Routine |
| Walk Dog |
| Go to Work |
| Lunch |
| Work Some More |
| End Workday |
| Walk Dog |
| Dinner |
| TV/Family Time |
| Evening Routine |
| Bedtime |

As you can see with this example, there's a lot of wiggle room within the daily schedule or time-blocking framework. Many people choose to insert prayer, meditation, or working out into their morning routine. Some opt to do this during their evening routine.

I've included space for "work time" that is open-ended and not itemized for a reason. Your work time will be completely different than another person's, and you probably have your own schedule or routine for your workday.

Think of your schedule, or your routine, as a personal assistant that is always there, keeping you on track. We will discuss this in greater detail in the Time Management component within the Peace Pyramid.

For now, it's time to pull out your map software to see how well it's getting you where you want to go. Exciting discoveries await you, I promise.

# Chapter 5

# Step 2: Program Your GPS

"If you do not know where you are going,
every road will get you nowhere."
—Lewis Carroll

I have a terrible sense of direction. I joke with friends and family that they should never ever take me on *The Amazing Race*, because I will get them lost. But just like *Dora the Explorer* teaches, we all need a map to help get us to where we want to go.

When I first started driving, I'd head one way on the main street and if I didn't hit my desired location after ten minutes or so, I'd just make a U-turn and head in the opposite direction. My glove compartment was filled with maps and printouts from the internet, but I never could seem to figure out how to read the squiggly lines all that well.

Thankfully, technology invented the global positioning system, or GPS.

And it was life-changing for me.

I'd like you to envision programming a GPS in your car when it comes to planning out your life.

In order to work properly, a GPS really only needs to know where you are right now and where you are headed.

There's no need to tell the GPS everywhere you've already been. The GPS isn't interested in hearing all about your past and where you've been or what roads you could have taken.

This is one of the major differences when it comes to life coaching versus therapy, and it's how I help my clients move forward with their goals and dreams. It's okay to have made mistakes in the past. I'm not judging you, nor should you be judged by anyone else, based on who you once were.

Today is your new beginning.

A great Buddhist quote comes to mind: "There are two best days to plant a tree. The first is twenty years ago, and the second is today."

## Programming Your Life GPS

You may have a goal of getting out of consumer debt, or paying off your home, or lowering your blood sugar so you don't need to take medication—those are all destinations that you can program into your metaphoric GPS.

For instance, I started writing online as a way to work from home while taking care of my children. That was my end goal: I wanted to find a legitimate way to make good money while continuing to be the primary caretaker for my three children.

So I urge you to take time to plot and plan exactly what you want out of life, and then figure out the path to get there. It may take a bit more time than you'd like, but if you stay the course and don't get distracted by too many detours along the way, you *will* get there, I promise.

But you need to keep moving forward in the right direction.

What is your end destination? A new home? A more fulfilling career? Early retirement? A strong and healthy body?

All of these destinations are absolutely possible (and probable!) when you take the time to purposefully plan.

Remember the metaphor of programming a GPS. If you're starting in San Francisco and want to head to Austin, you know that the journey will take a bit of time. And that's okay.

Along the way, if you hit some detours, or decide to take a side trip to hang out for a few days in Yosemite, that's okay. Your GPS will recalculate for you.

What you should *not* do when it takes a bit longer to get to Austin than you'd like is to turn around and go home.

That won't get you anywhere.

Instead, purposefully set your GPS and start heading toward your destination with the end in mind. And while you are programming or setting your metaphoric GPS, try to keep the five components of the Peace Pyramid in mind.

## Set Your Destination

Where are you headed in terms of Time Management, Health, Finances, Organization, and Relationships? In order to help me answer these questions, I envision a crystal ball and fast-forward to a faraway future date or age.

When I first began the practice of setting my GPS, I used Steph at age seventy as my end goal. I envisioned her laughing and crawling on the floor with her grandchildren and being strong enough to lift the dog in and out of the bathtub. I sometimes joke that since I make wise choices now, I'd like to loosen up a bit at that age and "eat and drink *all* the things."

I reserve the right to change my mind as I get closer to that age range, but for right now, the vision of me savoring a cocktail and greasy onion rings on the porch of our paid-for home while enjoying my family is enough for me to continue making wise choices in my forties. I'm happy to delay a current, momentary gratification in order to feel vibrant, healthy, and financially secure in my later years.

## Get off the Hamster Wheel

A former coaching client of mine once said that she felt like she was living the movie *Groundhog Day*—since there are always dishes to wash, laundry to fold, deadlines to meet, and children to drive to soccer practice. Because of these daily realities, she just can't seem to get ahead; she is essentially living the same day over and over again, without moving forward.

Do you ever feel that way too? I know I do! The monotony of daily tasks can start to feel almost comical.

A few years ago my eldest daughter adopted Penelope (Penny), a cute little fuzzy brown-and-white hamster. Penny spent hours each night running on her wheel. She exhausted herself, running in place—which meant that she was super happy to sleep all day, and would be crabby and prone to nip if you woke her up—since she'd been up all night "working."

No matter how hard she worked, or how long she ran, she stayed in the exact same place.

You are not destined to live out the life of a hamster. Please don't have this mindset.

It isn't "your lot in life" to feel unfulfilled, or to think "this is as good as it gets." It's also not too late. Nothing is "over"—you are not destined to stop growing or thriving or dreaming.

Take time to reprogram your GPS. And then keep moving forward.

## PACE Yourself

Remember that you don't need to overpack your days with tons of things to keep you busy nonstop. You are designed to be a human being, not a human *doing*.

Take time to plan out your day and be sure that you're prioritizing the actions needed to move toward your end goal. This may mean that you fold laundry while watching an instructional video, or wash dishes while on a conference call. It may mean that you take a client call in a parked car while at soccer practice.

You are in charge. You get to decide how you look at your day and how you schedule it out.

When this framework is in place, when you know where you're going and are continuously taking strides (baby steps count!) forward, you'll be able to pivot when life throws you curveballs (such as an unforeseen job loss, death in the family, natural disaster, or global pandemic).

I'd like to share an acronym (yes, another acronym!) I use when I find that my thoughts go a bit haywire and I think defeatist thoughts such as, *Ugh, this is taking too long. I will never get there. It's ridiculous how long this is taking. Everywhere I turn there's another block in the road.*

The acronym is PACE:

**P**eaceful
**A**cceptance of
**C**hanging
**E**vents

And my pace? It is to Go Slow.

Because the fact is, the only constant in life is change—and that's really hard for people to accept, me included.

Humans don't do well with things they can't control. Because the average lifespan is long, there's a good chance events will happen to you or to those you love that are completely out of your control, no matter how organized you are. Life comes with surprises we can't plan for. Just for starters:

- wildfire
- flood
- tornado
- hurricane
- sickness
- death
- disease
- divorce
- job loss
- earthquake
- burglary
- domestic violence

I hope these dreadful natural and man-made circumstances are not life experiences that you'll ever need to face or overcome. (But you could—and maybe you have already. The principles embedded within PACE apply to even the most challenging situations in life.) I list them because they are earth-shattering circumstances that some people need to withstand.

What about the other end of the spectrum? An out-of-stock item on Amazon? Heavy traffic? Running late to a movie? Accidentally missing a deadline at work? These are everyday mishaps that are not usually life-altering and don't warrant an out-of-proportion reaction. In other words, we can *let them go*.

Because the only constant we can really count on in life is that things will change. It's inevitable. But that doesn't mean change can't be positive. It's the only way civilization and our economy can continue to evolve and grow. Yes, it's a nice thought to wish that the empty lot down the street the neighborhood children play in will remain vacant, but in reality, it will probably become an apartment complex.

Unfortunate and disappointing things will happen as you move your way through life, but you are in charge of how you deal with these changes. And learning to PACE yourself through the peaceful acceptance of changing events will take you a long way toward where you want to go.

# Chapter 6

# Step 3: Stay Present and Positive

"When you arise in the morning, give thanks for the food and for the joy of living. If you see no reason for giving thanks, the fault lies only in yourself."
—Tecumseh

When you're able to pay attention to your surroundings and give thanks for all that you have, you'll begin to find that a peaceful serenity creeps into everything you do.

The best way to find things to be grateful for is to stay present in the Here and Now, instead of thinking of things that are coming up, or remembering things that have already happened.

## Narrate Your Life

If you find that you are having trouble maintaining a present state, my best suggestion is to start narrating your life. You can do this out loud, but you might get some funny looks if you aren't all alone.

This is what I mean: "I'm turning my alarm off right now. I'm going to silence my phone and walk into the bathroom. I'm looking at myself in the mirror. I will splash cold water on my face now. Huh, I look really good today. I'm going to turn around and head to the kitchen. I'm pulling out the coffee grounds. I'm looking for a measuring cup."

And so on.

Keeping a running dialogue of what is *actually happening* right this very moment can help you stay present and aware.

You won't need to do this forever, but it's a great exercise to begin each morning so you can begin to focus on the *wonderful things that **are already** in your life.

I like to practice my narration when I'm outside in the morning, walking the dog. I feel the cold air on my cheeks and look around to find a bird or airplane in the sky. I imagine where the bird or plane is flying. I breathe deeply and try to pinpoint the scent of honeysuckle or freshly cut grass.

You can do this, too.

Instead of thinking of all of the things on your to-do list during your morning shower, take the time to really sniff the scented soap and feel the differentiation between the water droplets.

Go Slow. Take your time.

I like to use the visual of a ruler when I'm sharing this concept with the students in my Simple Shortcuts to Peace course, or when I'm teaching a workshop. If you hold a ruler in your hand, look at only one measured inch. The measurements that are before your designated inch is the past, and the markings that are beyond your decided-upon inch is the future.

The only thing you can really "control" in your day-to-day life is what's happening in the Here and Now. If you find that your thoughts are drifting to past events or circumstances in your life, try to pivot to the present. The past already happened. There is no need to constantly replay or rehash what has already occurred.

Also, if you find that you spend a lot of time and brain energy worrying about the future, shift those thoughts to the Here and Now.

It's been said that worrying is like praying for things that you don't want. Instead, focus your thoughts on what is actively happening all around you.

## Push for Optimism

If you've ever owned a dog, you know firsthand what it's like to be always on the brink of being all in with optimism. When my dog, Sheldon, hears something fall onto the kitchen floor, he jumps up and runs into the room, even if he's been sound asleep clear on the other side of the house.

This is because three years ago, a meatball rolled off of a cookie sheet I was taking out of the oven and he was able to gobble it up.

Sheldon is an eternal optimist.

We live close to a pet food store that happily doles out treats to all of their four-legged customers. If we turn and head down the sidewalk toward the shopping plaza, Sheldon is convinced that we are going inside the pet store day or night, rain or shine. If we head that direction at all, he is certain the store will be open and he will be showered with hugs and treats.

He is wrong most of the time, yet he never loses hope.

How can you incorporate more optimism, hope, and gratitude into your life?

Many of my clients spend a few minutes each morning journaling and have maintained the practice of jotting down the things they are grateful for, along with some affirmations.

In 2018, researchers from the Greater Good Science Center published "The Science of Gratitude," a paper that outlined the following benefits that directly stem from practicing daily mindfulness and gratitude journaling.[14] Research participants reported:

- increased happiness and positive mood
- increased monetary savings
- more satisfaction with life
- being less materialistic
- being less likely to experience burnout
- better physical health
- better sleep
- less fatigue
- lower levels of cellular inflammation
- greater resiliency
- noticeable development of patience, humility, and wisdom

Embrace a practice of gratitude today, and I promise you'll begin to see a shift.

**"Keep your eyes on your own paper."**
**—classroom teachers all over the world**

## Ignore the Joneses

One of the best ways to feel good about your chosen path is to stop comparing what you are doing with others who are on a different path.

In yoga, a popular saying reminds participants to "keep your eyes on your own mat." This is practical advice because not only is yoga not a competition, but if you're too busy watching someone else's balanced pose, you'll immediately topple over.

Since you'll never know the intimate details of most people's bank accounts, relationships, or health, don't waste precious brain energy trying to match or one-up anybody else.

Theodore Roosevelt is said to have called comparison "the thief of joy." When you spend time contemplating what appears to be more success than another, it sucks away satisfaction with your own life. It's easy to make a snap judgment and think that the neighbor with the fancier car is somehow better or smarter than you.

This may be the case, but it also just doesn't matter.

Keep blinders on, as best you can, and pay attention to the game *you* are playing, not theirs.

In Thomas Stanley's fantastic book *The Millionaire Next Door*, he shares that most millionaires don't come across as all that flashy and instead shy away from conspicuous consumption because they'd rather not draw attention to themselves.[15]

When Adam and I were in the first few years of our marriage, I remember lamenting to him that it didn't "seem fair" that neighbors a few blocks away had a brand-new boat in the driveway and always seemed to dress their kids in expensive-looking clothes.

Years later, after we had moved away, I heard through the grapevine that they had bought all of those things on a home equity line of credit and when the market shifted, and their house wasn't worth as much, they needed to quickly liquidate and downsize.

Please don't fall victim to comparing your life to someone else's. Just like in elementary school, I'd like you to keep your eyes on your own paper.

Remember in the last section where I shared that my GPS was pointed to how Steph in her seventies wants to act and feel, and because of that it was okay to decide, on purpose, to delay quick gratification to have long-term satisfaction? This is true, but for a while, I forgot to have fun.

I had a self-chastising loop in my brain that said, "You'll have fun when the work is done." While this can be motivating for some when they are in the midst of a big work deadline or a home improvement project, it ended up backfiring for me because I never actually allowed myself to have *any* fun. I've since learned from that lesson and make a point of scheduling in fun and rewards (more on this in the Time Management section).

It's something I caution my clients about because the fact is, especially for many professions, there is *always* more work to do. So please, set ambitious goals, dream big, achieve milestone victories—and then reward yourself with some fun. You deserve to enjoy every bit of this life, and you can't keep putting off the good parts.

## Feel the Hard Feelings

Of course, life isn't always fun. It's okay to feel bad sometimes. It's okay to have uncomfortable feelings, to be a bit bored, and to feel anxiety bubble up. Humans aren't wired to always be on an even keel.

I teach the people I work with to "feel all of the feels— but then act on only the facts."

If you find that you feel uncomfortable or uneasy about something, sit with it for a while. Don't immediately try to distract yourself away from the uncomfortableness by numbing it out with TV, the internet, food, or alcohol.

One of the best side effects of taking the time to pause, and to mindfully be aware of your thoughts and feelings, is that you may very well become physically healthier.

We will discuss this further in the Health segment, but if you Slow Down and purposefully decide what you're going to eat, drink, and otherwise consume through your other senses, you'll find that your physical health will improve right along with your mental health.

## Limit Distractions

How much news do you watch on TV or online or read each day? Is watching the news, or following along through social media channels, helpful to you in your life?

Once I gave up watching the evening news and watching 24/7 cable news channels, I found that I suddenly had an awful lot more time in my day to tend to the backyard weeds or take Sheldon on another walk after dinner.

Purposely deciding to disengage from TV news does not mean that you're in the dark on important matters that happen globally or nationally. It's also important to pay attention to local weather notifications through text messaging or apps.

While I do scan the headlines each morning, I honestly don't miss watching televised news in the slightest, and you might also find this to be true.

Remember my earlier rewrite of the acronym FOMO, from Fear of Missing Out to Figure Only Yourself Out? If you're worried that you'll miss out on watercooler banter at work or at social events, that's okay. This concern is completely valid and is something you should decide for yourself.

Perhaps decide to only engage in scanning the headlines once or twice a day instead of checking each hour. Maybe only watch a bit of local news in the morning while dressing to be aware of the weather and traffic in your area.

You get to do you, but remember to actually decide what your limits are, and then stick to them. It's all too easy to get sucked into "one more segment after this next commercial break."

## Enjoy the Journey

**"A confident person enjoys the journey, the people they meet along the way and sees life not as a competition."**
**—Shannon Adler**

One of my favorite spiritual and personal development authors, Esther Hicks, shares in her seminars that the "joy is in the journey." This used to bother me when I was up all night with my first baby who refused to sleep and I felt like I was "doing it wrong" because I wasn't enjoying each and every second.

I remember being eager to fast-forward to the next phase of her childhood where she would (I hoped) sleep soundly and not need to be held all day long. I vividly recall balancing her on my lap, nursing, while trying to use the toilet because if I put her down she would scream so loudly that I worried the neighbors downstairs would be bothered and call child protective services. How could I possibly someday miss such a horrible circumstance?

Now, twenty years later, I do. I got through that challenging time and even more that came soon after. Time has a funny way of playing tricks on memories, and things that felt horrific at the time might seem sweet and have an air of nostalgia as we look back.

Pay attention to this. Go Slow and try your hardest when you're in the middle of a difficult time to remember that even while the days seem long, the years are short. They fly by. Soak in as many memories as you can, and try to stay present and enjoy the different steps and milestones along your lifelong path.

# Chapter 7

# Step 4: Take Action Daily (Ten Minutes Is All You Need)

"An object at rest remains at rest, and
an object in motion remains in motion."
—Sir Isaac Newton

You've heard all of the cliches about the importance of taking regular, daily action and moving step-by-step toward your goals. One bite of the elephant at a time. The journey of a thousand miles begins with a single step. Focus on the step in front of you, not the whole staircase. And so on.

Well, it just so happens that those are true. And that's the focus of this chapter. I'll share some of the insights and tools I've developed that have helped me, and many of my clients, to make gradual, measurable progress.

As I've written before, "Bit by bit, inch by inch, when you move slow, life's a cinch." Well, okay, it's not always a cinch, but embracing Slow Living can make even the biggest challenges look and feel much more manageable as you approach them a little at a time.

## Embrace 10-Minute Chunks

I'm a huge fan of timers. I'm also a huge fan of breaking things down into bite-sized chunks, or blocks, of time.

The fancy name for this is the Pomodoro Technique, a time-management method developed by Francesco Cirillo in the late 1980s. Pomodoro uses a timer to break down work into intervals, traditionally twenty-five minutes in length, separated by short breaks.

I found that when I was teaching preschool that the attention span of most two- to four-year-olds was about ten minutes. Because of this, I purposefully scheduled a 10-Minute Tidy cleanup time multiple times a day by setting the timer on my phone.

I'm much older now, but I find that when it comes to tasks that I don't particularly want to do, ten minutes continues to be my attention span.

The good news is that if you schedule a few 10-Minute Tidies throughout the day, you really can accomplish an awful lot.

And if you work together as a group or team, a *whole* bunch can get accomplished. For instance, in our family, we have five people. If we need to quickly get the house in order for company, all five of us working together creates fifty minutes' worth of cleaning.

That's a whole bunch of cleaning!

The easy-peasy approach is to set a timer for ten minutes (or tell Siri or Alexa to set the timer for you) and get to work.

**Tasks to do in 10-minute chunks** (set a timer, because it's easy to make tasks such as these expand exponentially!):

- Watch or read anything that motivates you to move forward on your goals.
- Go outside, sit in the garden, and feel the rain on your cheeks. Use this time to meditate and visualize your dream goal.
- Chat with someone you trust and vent out loud any frustrations you may be currently feeling that are keeping you from moving forward (i.e., running on a hamster wheel).
- Pick a room, a closet, or a cabinet, and start PROMing (purge, remove, organize, maintain).
- Push your body to its limits with extensive exercising, dancing, jumping, or running.
- Journal or daydream about any good times or memories that conjure feelings of warmth and happiness.
- Make a to-do list to plan out the next day.
- Write up a list of favorite dinners—include ten to twelve different meal ideas.
- Send an email to a friend you haven't heard from in a while.
- Unsubscribe to five marketing email lists.
- Create a playlist of your favorite uplifting songs.
- Clear your computer tabs and downloads folder.
- Sit in front of a mirror and talk to yourself in a kind and gentle way.

## Roll Out Your Mat

Yogis state that the hardest yoga move is to roll out your mat. This is because it's a lot tougher to get up and get moving than it is to stay sitting on the sidelines.

Channel Nike and do it anyway. Just do it.

Once you've got your mat out, it's pretty simple to sit on it and start stretching. Once you've got your running shoes laced up, it's not that hard to open the front door and put one foot in front of the other.

As you know by now, I like things slow, and while I really do feel like my natural state is to become one with the couch or my new down pillow-top mattress, I always feel better about myself if I accomplish the tasks I said I would.

I also have some pretty lofty dreams and goals and know that the only way I can get to them is to keep trudging forward, bit by bit.

## Make Sandcastles

The easiest way for me to get started on a large writing project is to envision a sandbox and each day add in another shovel of sand.

I try my hardest to just keep shoveling words into a blank word-processing document and get as many thoughts and ideas out of my head as I can. Once I've got a certain word count compiled, I go back and "make sandcastles" by editing and polishing the writing.

You can do this, too. Whatever the insurmountable task is that you have chosen to overcome or the dream you're trying to reach looks like, just keep shoveling the sand.

## Allow God and the Universe
## to Meet You Halfway

Authors Esther and Jerry Hicks share in their book *Ask and It Is Given* that when you begin to take baby steps toward your dreams and goals, the Universe or God will end up meeting you halfway.[16]

I saw this play out firsthand when I first appeared on *Rachael Ray*. I had emailed the show myself after making a perfect crème brûlée in the slow cooker. I bragged that I cracked the code to an easy restaurant-quality dessert with hardly any effort. My email worked and I got to fly to New York and appear on the show.

What I didn't know was that one of my readers watched the show and was so impressed she asked her husband, who worked for ABC, to also watch the segment. He then decided to reach out to ABC's publishing arm, Hyperion, and I was asked to write my first cookbook.

This was not anything I could have orchestrated on my own and is an example of the Hicks' definition of the Universe meeting me halfway.

Travis, a stay-at-home dad of three, reached out to me a year or so ago for some life coaching. He was frustrated with the housing market and reported that homes in his preferred neighborhood were being sold for $100,000 to $250,000 over the asking price. He said that because of this, he and his wife would never be able to afford the required 20 percent down payment.

I asked what his realtor and mortgage broker had to say. He answered that he and his wife hadn't met with or hired either because they weren't yet ready.

With some nudging and helpful guidance from me, I asked him to take those next steps—secure a realtor and ask a mortgage broker to assess their finances and see what type of loan they could be pre-approved for.

Six months or so later, Travis emailed me to say that the realtor they met with had a lead on a house that was going to be sold by the owner, and since they already had proven to the mortgage broker they could make the monthly payments, they didn't need to secure such a large down payment.

That's pretty darn awesome!

# Chapter 8

# Step 5: Fine Tune as Needed

"It's the courage to continue that counts."
—Winston Churchill

I like to garden. Many people enjoy growing vegetables or fun and colorful flowers, but right now, I spend many hours a week working on my front lawn.

It might sound a bit boring to some, but I garner immense pleasure by taking the time to mow (I have a manual, nonmotorized rotary mower, so I can mow at 6 a.m. without disturbing the neighbors!) at a high height, and by using large garden scissors to trim the edges.

It would be a lot faster to hire someone to use a power mower or edger, but I'm not in a rush. I enjoy the act of maintaining my lawn.

I spend a lot of time researching organic lawn fertilizers and deciding the optimum height for mowing depending on how much moisture is in the ground and what the humidity level is in the air.

Because of this, I'm able to fulfill California's drought requirements and I don't need to water my lawn all that often.

Playing in my yard and researching grass makes me happy. It's one of my hobbies, is good for my mental health, and I view it as a form of self-care.

Sometimes in the afternoon, I spread out a beach towel and "comb" through the grass with my fingers and try to find the beginning sprouts of crabgrass, clover, or a dandelion. Since I do this so very often, it's now a struggle to find an errant weed.

There is a home in the neighborhood with a yard full of weeds. It would take an extraordinary amount of work, and probably a rototiller, to free that front yard from weeds.

I'd like you to think of your life as a field of green grass.

A really beautiful and organically maintained field of grass. One that the neighbors notice when they walk by, and a lawn that no one would dream of letting their dog pee on.

When a thought, activity, or person pops up that doesn't fit into the lovely green aesthetic of the life you are trying to maintain, pluck it. Don't let this errant thought, activity, or person "go to seed" and spread all over your yard.

If you find that your life isn't as green and lush as you'd like, and you've got too many weeds, that's okay. You can work to fix it. And while busting out a tiller might sound like a good idea, there are calmer and gentler ways to get your life back on track—many of which we're going to explore along the way.

You already have a head start, because you've read this far. Start paying attention to the thoughts that are feeding your feelings, and if the thoughts aren't helping you to move forward in your life, change them.

If you find that you aren't able to do this all on your own, please talk to your doctor or look toward investing in professional help.

Remember the metaphor of setting your GPS. A navigation system doesn't need to know where you've already been. It just helps you get to where you're going.

# Part 3

# The Peace Pyramid: The Reward

If you're anything like me, you may have scoured the bookstore and library and read multiple books that tout empty promises or pie-in-the-sky affirmations depicting a carefree life where everything is hunky-dory.

I spent the good part of my twenties and thirties listening to books on tape, watching YouTube videos, and creating "master schedules" with color-coded Post-it Notes.

I thought that each new self-help or personal development book would be the key to uncovering a completely organized life, free from troubles or trauma. I wasted a lot of precious time and money.

One of the cool side effects of beginning my website was that I suddenly had a relationship with tens of thousands of readers from all over the world. These were real people— just like me—who were just trying to get through the day.

As I started answering their emails about cooking and slow cooker recipes, I noticed I was receiving questions that had nothing to do with cooking or meal planning. Instead, I started fielding inquiries about time management and household organization and parenting struggles.

After researching the answers to these questions, I began formatting my discoveries in a way that could be replicated by others—regardless of age or life situation.

The Peace Pyramid, which I introduced briefly in Part 1, was developed as an answer to the many questions I had as I transitioned from young to older-and-wiser adulthood, and as a resource to help as many people as possible who may also have questions, worries, and insecurities.

I hope you find it useful.

## Where Are You Going?

As stated earlier, when you embark upon your journey through life, it's important to know where you're headed. Together, we are going to map out a plan and point your metaphoric GPS to the top of the Peace Pyramid.

Many self-help books and mentors claim that all you have to do to experience inner peace is to meditate. Or start a gratitude journal. Or have more self-discipline or willpower. Or take up yoga. Or say hundreds of affirmations as soon as you get up in the morning.

The problem with these types of books or programs is that in real life, most people don't have the luxury to sit around and navel-gaze and contemplate the state of the world.

So we put it off.

We say things to ourselves like:

"I can't have peace right now because we have credit card debt."

"I can't feel calm because I keep fighting with my mom and sister."

"I don't deserve to feel tranquility because I don't have any willpower to stick to my diet plan."

I know this. I lived this. I get it.

We learned in elementary school geometry that the most stable of all man-made structures is a pyramid. And the reason a pyramid is so strong, steady, and stable is because a lot of time and care is taken to thoughtfully design and construct the foundation.

Most personal development and self-help programs unfortunately start backward—they begin at the top without taking the time to build a solid foundation. Lots of books and programs ask readers to hope and wish and pray for peace, which can sometimes make people feel as if they have failed if they don't achieve great things.

*If only I had dreamt harder, my life would be complete!*

Many spend most of their time daydreaming and fantasizing about the future instead of taking tangible action, which results in massive discouragement and feelings of failure.

Dreaming is wonderful.

I *love* daydreaming and could easily whittle away hours a day painting beautiful images of happiness and tranquility in my mind. Unfortunately, this is where many people get stuck. They have the dreaming part down pat, but not the action steps to ensure their dreams materialize!

That's why I've written this book as a step-by-step guide, with the imagery of a pyramid at the very core of all the advice and teaching.

We will work together to ensure that you have the strongest foundation possible.

And trust me, I know foundations. I'm the daughter of an architect and am married to a structural engineer!

## Creating a Strong and Stable Foundation

If we're lucky, life is long. There is no reason whatsoever to not have the ability to enjoy every last bit of it. Unfortunately, hardships happen. Sickness, death, loss of job—these things are real and are all part of the human experience.

That's why in order to live the best version of your life, you need to have your core foundation as strong as possible—otherwise you may inadvertently build a house of cards.

# Chapter 9

# Your Path to Peace: Time Management

"Time is really the only capital that any
human being has, and the only
thing he can't afford to lose."
—Thomas Edison

The very first component in the Peace Pyramid is Time Management. It took me a while to figure out that in order to live the life of my dreams, to have a good marriage or a good relationship with my kids, to have a balanced budget, an organized linen closet, or even keep my weight in check, I needed to figure out how to effectively manage my day-to-day tasks.

It's a bit like the chicken and the egg.

When you're able to effectively manage your time, you create space for activities that bring you joy, relaxation, and fulfillment, which leads to a sense of peace within yourself. Also, when you feel at peace, you are better equipped to manage your time wisely because you aren't bogged down by stress, anxiety, or distractions.

If we want to put structures in place so we can feel at peace, we need to start with time management. The good news is that this version of time management is designed for normal people and not for super humans who are trying to cram more and more into an already overfilled day.

## Prioritize Your Schedule

Remember from our PROM acronym that the first step to living a Slow Life is to declutter all that doesn't serve you. This is absolutely applicable to your daily schedule and calendar as well. One of the best ways to do this is to start prioritizing how you spend your time.

The following example is sometimes shared in time management seminars or workshops, and I first learned about it through a recorded seminar I found on YouTube led by Stephen Covey.[17] I'd like to share it with you as a way to prioritize your daily to-dos.

Once you have a big vision of what is important in your life, and what isn't, you can start to provide structure in your day-to-day life.

If the empty jar is your life, and you're told that all of the parts of your life need to get placed into the jar, the only way to cram them all in is to start with the big rocks first.

*The big rocks are your top priority.*

The pebbles are the next thing to go into the jar, and finally, the sand can get sprinkled into the nooks and crannies.

In your life, the big rocks might be yourself (physical and mental health), your immediate family (children and your spouse or significant other), and perhaps your day job (or how you make money).

Pebbles might represent coworkers, in-laws, other relatives, friends, neighbors, and hobbies.

The sand is peripheral filler such as TV-watching, surfing the web, interactions with casual acquaintances, reading the news, material possessions, traffic, and anything else you end up filling your day or life with.

*If you aren't careful to pack your jar thoughtfully and with intention, it can easily be filled first with sand and little rocks—which will not leave enough room for your big rocks.*

Take the time to pause and think about how you fill your "jar of life."

Most people find that they are moving through life too quickly, are caught up in the MORE MORE MORE Hustle Culture, and are left feeling frantic because they don't have enough time or space to do the things they really want to do.

If you fill your life with too much "stuff" or "sand," the people, things, experiences, and activities that mean the most to you won't have enough room to fit into your "jar."

I don't want that to happen to you. I want you to live a calm, peaceful, and tranquil life filled with purpose and abundance.

## Don't Overpack Your Schedule

You deserve to live the life of your dreams. So let's decide on a few (just a few!) key things (the big rocks!) that need to get accomplished each day. Then, add in a couple of pebbles.

It's also okay to schedule in free time, naps, and chillaxing time. Taking care of your physical and mental health is always considered "big rocks." There is no need to schedule in sand. Sand always finds a way to sneak in, even on what seem to be the most packed days.

Let's get an action plan in place.

Here's how it began for me. I first started reading time management books in 2001 when my eldest daughter was born.

I was exhausted all the time and couldn't figure out how I could be a good mom to her, a good wife to my husband, and a good employee at work. I was running two nonprofit childcare centers for the county department of family and social services. One of those childcare centers was at a homeless shelter.

I had deadlines and meetings I needed to think about when I was at home, and when I was at work I worried about baby sleep cycles, nursing on demand, and trying to remember to call and check in with my parents and grandparents.

I was certain that if I were just more organized, or if I just got a better night's sleep, or if I just lost that final twelve (okay, twenty-seven) pounds, or if I could just make more money, everything would be okay.

But it wasn't. I wasn't okay.

So I started scouring the shelves at the local library, searching for answers.

And what I noticed was that many of the time-management books were written for businessmen from an era when the breadwinner worked outside of the house all day and had less responsibility for the day-to-day running of the family home. It was appropriate and acceptable when they were written, but they didn't really feel applicable to me.

The books assumed that the only thing the businessmen needed to do was to find time in their day to get more work done.

And that wasn't helpful to me. I was (and still am) a regular person trying my best to function in the twenty-first century.

## Maximizing the 5 to 9

Regular, everyday people want to perform well not only at work but also at home, and have an appropriate work-life balance.

In order to help achieve this, we need to make a mental switch: You don't work from 9 to 5.

No. You actually work from *5 to 9*.

Why? Because there's no point in trying to cram every last thing into a traditional eight-hour workday. That's a recipe for insanity.

So instead, decide from here on out that your workday—your *entire* workday—is between the hours of 5 a.m. and 9 p.m.

Hear me out. I know you're thinking, *Hey, Steph, I don't want to get up at 5 a.m. every day. That doesn't sound like Slow Living to me! That sounds like setting an alarm and getting up at the crack of dawn and that sounds dreadful. Try again.*

I know.

I don't want to have to get up at 5 a.m. either.

But I also don't want to feel defeated the second I open my eyes in the morning.

The very best way I can possibly get my day started on the right foot is to center myself for an hour or two before anybody needs me to do anything for them. For *me*, that means 5 a.m.

Because my children (and the dog!) wake up around 6:30 a.m. and I need to leave the house for work at 7:30 a.m., the best way for me to feel calm, centered, and as if I am in control of my time is to get up at this time.

If you work from home and have a flexible work schedule, or you homeschool and your kids sleep in until 10 a.m. each day, then you don't need to get up at 5 a.m. Instead, get up at 8 a.m. No problem.

But from coaching countless people over the years, I can tell you without a doubt that the very best advice I can possibly give is to get up an hour or two before you need to do anything in any way for anyone except for you.

Because this way you're paying yourself first.

## Pay Yourself First

Perhaps you've heard from financial and money management advisers that the best way to save money and create wealth is to pay yourself first (this is true, and will be discussed in full in an upcoming chapter). I'm suggesting that the best way to start off your day is to pay yourself first when it comes to time allotment.

How does this work?

Well, this means I can skip checking email or any social networking, because if I do that, or if you do that, it means that you're already starting the day on someone else's agenda.

And that's not right.

What does a typical schedule look like? For me, this is what happens.

I usually start my day by getting the coffee ready, and then I make sure all of the dishes from the drainer or dishwasher are put away and there is nothing left anywhere in the kitchen or main living part of the house that didn't get put away before bed.

This takes me about seven to ten minutes, total. By then my coffee is ready and smells great, and so I take those first few sips while walking slowly through the quiet house.

I use this time to reflect, meditate, and journal. Many of my friends and clients use this time to pray. I love this quiet reflection time—it's not structured, it's not rushed, it's just me and the birds chirping.

I like to sit on my yoga mat with my journaling worksheet and coffee and stretch, write, and sip. I don't have a specific sequence of yoga stretches that I follow, I just move according to what my body needs and wants each particular day. This free-flow meditative journaling time runs about thirty minutes.

From there, I either do a workout in the garage with some dumbbells on a weight bench, or I go on a short run around the neighborhood.

After my workout, the clock reads close to 6:30 a.m., which means it's my turn to go upstairs to take a shower and get dressed. I also ensure that the bed is made and any laundry left in the bathroom gets carried downstairs to plop into the washing machine.

At 7 a.m. I wake up Sheldon and take him for a walk. While I walk the dog, I usually chat on the phone with my girlfriend Jennifer.

These are the "big rocks" of my morning routine. Other stuff happens in this timeframe: lunches get made, texts are answered, homework is signed, and figuring out what's for dinner happens. But that kind of stuff is going to happen no matter what. I still decide on purpose what my big rocks are going to be and schedule them in.

My kids usually get themselves breakfast, but when I had little ones I'd set them up with a yogurt and a piece of toast before heading off to get myself dressed and completely ready to leave the house for the day. At 7:30 a.m. I'm in the car, headed to work.

And this is my morning.

I get an *awful* lot done in two and a half hours, and in doing so it really sets me up for the entire day.

For a while, I tried to be more "relaxed" in the morning and just let things happen without scheduling. Guess what? It felt horrible.

When I worked from home, I experimented with getting up at 7 a.m. with the kids, but I found that I always felt a bit behind and I'd end up taking them to school in my pajamas and without brushing my teeth. This seemed appropriate at the time. I'd just find a way to squeeze in all the stuff I had to do while the kids were at school.

Except it just didn't work that way. I felt frenzied and frantic because instead of setting myself up first and foremost for success, I waited for outside circumstances to dictate my actions.

So now I start my days off on the right foot: I work out, tidy the kitchen, start a load of laundry, and get completely dressed (including a touch of makeup!) before leaving the house.

Is it perfect? No, but it works well for me, and it starts the day off in a productive way and allows me to get my brain centered and my body nurtured.

Will this daily morning routine work for everybody?

Absolutely. Not.

If you have a newborn in the house or are not sleeping soundly, this won't work—your sleep absolutely should come first.

Stuff happens.

Life happens.

There are going to be days when someone is sick, including you, and other days when you're up at night with a little one who had a nightmare.

I get it.

We're not after perfection here. We are after tiny tweaks and changes that can become *big results*, bit by bit, over time.

Let's pause for a minute here, and SLOW down.

I'd like you to jot down your own version of a morning routine where you can pay yourself first.

And remember, do it for your own stage of life and what makes you feel the best. Chances are you don't need as much time to do the things on your list as you think you do.

One of our family's favorite movies is *Daddy Daycare* starring Eddie Murphy, which includes a line about how children thrive with a structure in place—similar to how a vine clings to a trellis for support as it grows and gains strength.

That concept applies to more than just children. You can use your daily schedule as a support system. Stick to it and gain strength. When you begin to see results from saying no and sticking to your boundaries, you can loosen up and not cling so tightly to the schedule. After you've paid yourself first, you can move on to getting the things you have to do squared away.

So, please utilize the first step in Slowing Down by decluttering your calendar from all the things that really aren't necessary to help you move forward toward living out the life of your dreams.

We will do this by learning how to properly delegate and practicing the art of saying "no."

# How to Properly Delegate

If you are doing something that's taking a lot of your time that would be best spent by getting this task off of your daily calendar, then you should delegate it. And delegation doesn't necessarily mean hiring outside help.

Sure, you can delegate the deep cleaning by calling in a housekeeping service (I discuss this fully in the Organization chapter), and you can delegate washing your car by driving it through the car wash around the corner.

But I'm not trying to get you to spend money here—mostly I'm trying to figure out where your time is best spent.

For instance: birthday party gifts. Are you going to need to shop for ten to twelve birthday party gifts this year for children in the third grade?

Delegate—and you can delegate it easily *right now* by just going on Amazon and buying twelve of the board game *Clue*. It's gender-neutral, it's a great game, and it's reasonably priced.

NEXT.

Do you always host Thanksgiving dinner at your house? Great. Delegate. Write up your guest list and then write a side dish, appetizer, or beverage by each and every person's name.

When you send out the invitations, write something like: *Hey Kelly, we're going "structured potluck" this year to help alleviate the stress of the holidays. This is my famous cornbread stuffing recipe. Will you please bring it along? I'll make sure to have your favorite wine! You're the best!*

And there you go. This is how to properly delegate.

## The Art of Saying No

While I joke that there's an art to it, there really isn't. All you need to do is say NO.

Remember that the first step to Slow Living is to declutter—you can't keep cramming more and more in and expect to feel peaceful. Agree to fewer things to place on your calendar and daily schedule.

And then say no. Say no to planning the PTA fundraiser. Say no to your mothers' club annual tea.

Say no to *everything* that doesn't fully bless your family.

If you are saying yes to things out of guilt, then you're sending out a message to the Universe that you are a doormat. And your children are watching. Do you want them to grow up thinking that they aren't in control of their day-to-day actions?

Do you want them to learn that the way to keep friends is to break themselves by going above and beyond each and every time because of some weird internal competition?

Of course, you don't.

Just. Say. No.

No explanation is needed, but if you really feel you must say something other than no, then simply say, "Thank you for the invite, but we just have too much going on right now to commit to anything else."

And that's it! Who can argue with that?!

Later down the line, when you get good at saying no, and you feel like you do have time in your family's busy schedule to do more things, guess what? There will always be opportunities to get involved again with service in your community. But please don't make yourself or your family martyrs until you have gotten your life and time in order.

Saying no now does not mean no forever. It just means for right now.

If we apply the Mindset + Action + Consistency = Success formula to time management, you may find it helpful to schedule in calendar assessment on a regular basis. I find that to stay on task with my goals and ideas, I need to consistently revisit my calendar to ensure that I'm not accidentally placing too many things on it that aren't helping me move forward in my personal and professional goals.

I've created a tool that I use to help with this that you may also find useful. You can download a copy of my daily journaling worksheet and a blank 5 to 9 calendar on my website at stephanieodea.com/daily. Saying yes to that opportunity is one I promise you'll be glad you did.

# Chapter 10

# Wellness from Within: Health

"Take care of your body. It's the only
place you have to live."
—Jim Rohn

I thought for a long time about which section of the Peace Pyramid should pair with Time Management before settling on Health.

I chose it for a reason, because you are no good to anyone—not to your kids, not to your spouse, not to your work, and certainly not to yourself—if you don't love, honor, and nurture your brain and your body.

I can't even possibly express to you how important it is to take charge of your health. Many of the people who come to me for help self-identify as caregivers in some way. Some are teachers, others are nurses, many are parents, and quite a few consider themselves squarely within the "sandwich generation"—because not only are they caring for their own children, they are also caring for their aging parents in some capacity.

You can't function as a caregiver properly if you don't have a handle on your own health and well-being.

So what does that mean? It means you are eating right, you're exercising, you understand what's going on with your energy and your hormones, you're sleeping properly, you're regularly seeing the doctor and dentist, and you honor your mental health.

I know, it sounds like a lot. It's tough being an adult!

But here's the thing: you wouldn't dream of skipping regularly scheduled medical appointments for your newborn, but statistically after the six-week postpartum checkup, many moms stop going to the doctor for themselves. It's time to fix this.

There are 6 Key Components to Health:

1. Diet
2. Movement
3. Sleep
4. Hormones
5. Regular Medical Appointments
6. Mental Health

Let's take a closer look at each one of them and the vital role they play in your overall health.

## 1. DIET

It's a four-letter word, but it shouldn't be!

My very first paid job (outside of babysitting) was working in the education department at the San Francisco Zoo. Once in a while I got to lead the nature shows in the

Wildlife Theater. The first question I was asked whenever I introduced an animal to the audience was, "What's its diet? What does it eat?"

And that's all a diet is. It's what you normally eat.

Nobody would dream of thinking that a koala is on this or that new fad because its diet is eucalyptus leaves. No. That's just what a koala's diet is. Koalas mostly eat eucalyptus leaves. Do koalas sometimes eat oranges and alfalfa hay and watermelon rinds? Sure. But I think we can all agree that a koala's natural diet is eucalyptus leaves.

So why do we call a terribly restrictive and formulaic way of eating a DIET? Why don't we call it a six-week test?

Because if you go on a six-week or a twelve-week or a WHATEVER formatted FOOD TEST and then go EXACTLY BACK TO EATING the way you were before, then you most certainly have not changed your diet.

So, that's all I'm asking of you.

Take care of yourself. Be aware. Be deliberate.

Figure out what nutritional eating plan works for you and then stick to it.

Almost every day a reader or a client will write about how she lost a ton of weight following this or that eating plan, but then gained it all back when she went back to eating "normally."

That's the thing. You have to create a "new normal" for yourself. And the new normal is to be a happy, healthy, well-rounded person who is a good role model for yourself and your family.

That's it. It's not someone who needs six-pack abs or looks like an online influencer in order to feel good about herself. It's someone who is aware of what she is eating and drinking and knows that what she puts into her body affects her well-being.

She knows that while she'd rather have three glasses of wine at night, she sleeps better and is a nicer person if she limits it to one five-ounce serving.

Since we all know how much I love acronyms—let's make one for the word *diet*. From now on, when you want to eat something, think of this new acronym for diet:

**D**o
**I**
**E**at
**T**his?

When you're in a good mood, simply look only within and decide with purpose what your main diet is—what do you eat? Many people find great success by writing out their food plan before the day gets super underway. If you've decided to time-block your days, you can also pre-plan what you are going to eat.

## Food Intolerances and Allergies

We happen to keep a gluten-free household because we have celiac disease in the family. We also have a nut allergy in our extended family and have additional family members with food intolerances. Because of this, I have gotten very good at reading nutrition labels.

Use the tools that are at your disposal. If you aren't sure what the calorie content or carb allotment a certain food has, look it up. We are so lucky to be living in a time when we can have a computer in our back pocket. Use it.

If you need to eat a certain way to make your body feel its best, you're already slowing down because you aren't haphazardly popping something into your mouth without true awareness. Decide to look at this as a good thing, not a hindrance.

## Calories In / Calories Out

There are tons of fad eating plans on the market, and really, they are all formatted essentially the same way. If you take in more calories than you expend, you'll gain weight. If you take in fewer calories than you expend, you'll lose. If you take in exactly what you put out, you'll stay the same.

And that's really about it. It's been studied to death, and you can certainly look up loads of medical research, but a pound of fat is right around 3,500 calories, or units of energy.

That means that all you'd need to do is shave off about 500 calories a day from what you normally consume to lose one pound a week.

Sounds easy, right?

It's not. If it were easy, the weight loss industry wouldn't be worth approximately $300 billion annually.

The calorie math makes sense, and if you were a spreadsheet or a computer program, this would be great.

But you're not.

You're a real human with ups and downs and all-arounds, and that's what makes a simple math equation not a realistic game plan for most humans.

Let's go back to the initial premise of this book, which is to go SLOW: Simply Look Only Within. What is it you're trying to achieve with your health?

This is about being the best version of *you*. No one else—you!

You can absolutely feel your best without six-pack abs or wearing skinny jeans or having whatever a "thigh gap" is.

It's not healthy for your brain or your body to always be striving for a certain aesthetic look that may very well not be achievable or applicable for your body or genetic makeup.

Linda Bacon is a researcher and the author of *Health at Every Size: The Surprising Truth About Your Weight.* She holds a PhD in physiology with a focus on nutrition and weight regulation.

The concept of Health at Every Size (HAES) is about "taking care of your body without worrying about whether you're 'too' big or small," Bacon says. "People might think they can tell who's fit and who's not by looking at them, but in fact, it's trickier than that. Lots of people are fat and fit—many avid dancers, runners, lifters, and sports team members are big to start with and stay that way. They tend to be far healthier than thin people who don't move around much or eat a nutritious mix of foods. Saying everybody needs to be the same weight is like saying all people should be the same height."[18]

My hope is that by taking the time to really look within, you'll find answers that make you feel strong and empowered to feed, nourish, and cherish your body—regardless of how it looks.

## Sugar/Carbs/Alcohol

When I first sit down with a client who wants to take control of her health, she inevitably asks me, "Should I give up sugar? Or all carbs? What about alcohol?"

I can't answer any of those questions for you.

Only *you* know if you may be hindered in your health goals and aspirations by these types of foods. My best suggestion is that when you're in a good mood, make out a game plan for yourself (Step 2 of Slow Living).

Where do these foods fit in? Do you need to declutter them for a while in order to meet your goals (Step 1 of Slow Living)? Maybe not forever, but for a bit to see how you respond?

The 58th episode of the *Slow Living* podcast is entitled "Sober Curiosity." In this episode, I ask listeners to think about whether their alcohol consumption is helping them or hindering them when it comes to meeting their personal and professional goals. It's a question you as a reader can consider as well. Get curious. You are your own best judge of what's right and wrong for you.

Two of my favorite researchers about sugars and carbs are Dr. Jason Fung and Gary Taubes. Among their works, Dr. Fung has written *The Obesity Code* and *The Diabetes Code*, and Taubes has written *Why We Get Fat* and *Good Calories, Bad Calories*. These books are well-researched and explain the science behind why sugar is highly addictive and how simply cutting calories may not work for all body types.

## 2. Movement

Whenever I think of the word *movement*, I envision the dancing lemurs in the movie *Madagascar*. And that's a good thing. Because when you decide to "move it" and incorporate more movement into your day, not only are you as happy as a leaping lemur, but you're also automatically deciding to respect your body.

Your body was made to move, and remember, we are in a "use it or lose it" relationship with our bodies.

Movement is also so much easier to measure and track than weight. As Dr. Linda Bacon writes, weight really doesn't have all that much to do with health and overall wellness.

Let's stop here for a moment. I'm going to repeat that: movement, exercise, and working out have NOTHING TO DO WITH LOSING WEIGHT.

I am not talking about exercising to burn calories or to fit into a certain pair of jeans. I'm talking about moving your body so your joints work properly, your muscles are engaged and active, and your heart, lungs, and brain are all in proper working order.

If, when you decide to actively get up and *move* each and every day, you just so happen to lose weight? Then great. But that's not the goal here.

The goal is to live a long, healthy, and happy life and to be a *great* role model for your children.

The US Surgeon General has recommended that the general population should get about 150 minutes of heart-beating-faster-than-normal movement a week and log about 10,000 steps a day. Let's dissect this a bit.[19] A total of 150 minutes a week works out to 21.4 minutes a day.

What are your thoughts on that? Does that seem doable? If you hike for an hour on Sunday, does this count?

Yes. Yes, it does. What we are aiming for is a deliberate movement that raises your heart rate for about twenty minutes or so a day.

According to the results of a Centers for Disease Control survey announced in January of 2023, only 28 percent of respondents met this 150 minutes a week suggested benchmark.[20] The survey also found that almost a third of Americans don't exercise at all—which is worrisome, since a sedentary lifestyle can lead to an increased risk of disease or other health conditions later in life.

How do we fix this? It's time to go back to the Time Management component of the Peace Pyramid. You've got to deliberately plan to be active.

It really doesn't matter how you achieve this—join a gym, don't join a gym. Whatever works for you and is *sustainable* (there it is again—that's the word of the day!) for the long term, that's what you need to do. Remember, we are not working out to lose weight here. We are working out to honor our bodies and our health with movement.

It doesn't matter how much you work out. You're not going to outwork a bad diet. If you don't understand proper nutrition and calories in versus calories out, then rewind and go back to the beginning of this chapter where we talk about what your normal eating plan or "diet" is.

I'm again going to repeat myself: YOU CANNOT OUT-RUN OR OUT-WORKOUT A BAD DIET.

What you put into your body counts.

This is *your life*.

And you want to live for a *long time*.

So don't procrastinate. Start now, even if it's a tiny step forward. The everyday things you do make up the patchwork quilt of a life well-lived.

Exercise, especially cardio like running or going for a brisk walk, can also recharge your brain if you're in a creative slump. I often come in from a run or a long walk with Sheldon and go straight to my computer so I can brain-dump all the inspiration that came to me while I was out running or walking.

## Up Your NEAT

Here's another helpful acronym—NEAT:

**N**on-
**E**xercise
**A**ctivity
**T**hermogenesis

This may sound complicated and science-y, but it simply means all the stuff you do outside of formal exercise:

- Standing instead of sitting
- Taking the stairs instead of the elevator/escalator

- Walking the dog into the yard instead of merely opening the dog door
- Unloading groceries
- Gardening
- Stretching between switching tasks
- Fidgeting
- Tapping your feet to music

Anything you do with your body that causes it to incorporate more movement and therefore get a bit stronger, more flexible, and stable counts. All in all, this is why you should just **MOVE**. It's the only way to keep you alive and kicking for the long haul.

## 3. Sleep

Adults need between seven and nine hours of sleep a night. That's an average of eight hours, although some adults need as much as nine or ten hours.

We've all heard this.

We all know this.

I'm not going to beat you over the head. You know what amount of sleep works the best for you. When you're well rested, your body and your brain simply work better.

If you have a hard time falling asleep at night, then make a plan to figure out what's going on. Are you drinking too much alcohol or caffeine? Or both? This affects sleep. Are you worrying about work and other life stresses too much? This affects sleep. Are you uncomfortable in your bed, or do you have back pain that's keeping you awake? Figure it out.

People who get a good night's sleep live longer and have better mental health. You can't be at your peak performance if you aren't resting enough at night to replenish your cells.

Also, studies have shown that napping throughout the day can really help productivity, provided that you don't fall into too deep of a sleep cycle.

I've always been the kind of person who can catnap pretty easily, so I have no issues with lying down on the couch and falling asleep during an episode of *Paw Patrol*. I've always been able to nap. Even in college I would go out to my car between classes, set the alarm on my phone for twenty to thirty minutes, and fall asleep.

My husband, on the other hand, can sometimes get a bit cranky if he falls asleep during the day because he can't just catnap; he slips into a very deep sleep cycle and then has a hard time snapping out of it.

Your brain is the most "awake" and "alive" thirty to sixty minutes after you wake up.

This is helpful to me as a writer, because if I'm in a writing slump or just don't feel creative, I can go lie down and the back of my mind seems to work on my stumbling block while I'm asleep. More often than not, I can get over my block after a nap.

## Getting Tested for Sleep Apnea

For a long time, I felt like I just couldn't get enough sleep. It seemed as soon as I woke up I began doing mental math to calculate when I could go back to bed or schedule a nap.

I brought this up to my doctor a few times and was met with dismissive retorts such as "Welcome to motherhood!" and "This is just how it is in your forties!"

It wasn't until I went away on a girls' weekend and a friend told me that my snoring kept her up that I thought to google "tired all the time and snoring." My rudimentary research pointed to sleep apnea. When I went back to my doctor and asked for a sleep study, I learned that I had an apnea score that showed I stopped breathing forty-five to sixty times a night.

That's a lot!

After getting fitted with a CPAP machine, I now sleep quite well and can get into deep, restful sleep each night.

# 4. Hormones

When I first started teaching and coaching, it was somewhat taboo to talk about hormones and how they can dominate (and sometimes dictate) a big portion of your day-to-day life. I was even chastised once for being anti-feminist for bringing the subject up in a women's seminar!

Thankfully, the tide has turned and now it's commonplace to discuss hormones and their profound effect on women's bodies. Women have cycles for about thirty years, and during that time much of what we do comes right back to hormones.

If you're not in this demographic, feel free to skip this section. If this does sound like you, please read on.

Women have three kinds of dominant hormones coursing through their bodies: estrogen, testosterone, and progesterone. During the first half of our monthly cycle, estrogen is the most dominant, and in the second half, progesterone is the most dominant.

I'm going to give you a down-and-dirty, non-endocrinologist explanation about the difference between these hormones that are responsible for pretty much everything that happens in our day-to-day lives.

First off, we should assume that you're not chemically altering your hormones with birth control pills or any other form of hormone replacement or hindering therapy. If you are, this will still be applicable to you, just maybe on a less intense scale.

I usually find that women in their late thirties to mid-forties begin complaining about their hormones and start researching and asking, "What's wrong with me?!" There's nothing wrong. This is what is supposed to happen. Here's the thing:

Research shows that the three key hormones that rise and fall throughout your monthly cycle—estrogen, testosterone, and progesterone—affect your mood, energy, food cravings, memory, romantic life, friendships, whether or not you feel social, and virtually *every other part* of your day.

This is something to pay attention to because if you are feeling discouraged for not being as productive as you were the week prior, it's not your fault.

If you find that you have more energy at certain times of the month, plan for it. You're not designed to function at maximum capacity each and every day, and you're not a spreadsheet. You can't expect that every day, week, or month will be the same. Listen to your body and honor its whims and natural energy peaks and valleys.

If possible, try to schedule large projects or strenuous activities during a peak energy cycle.

For more information about this, I highly recommend the MyHormonology.com website and the book *28 Days* by Gabrielle Lichterman. Since I first began teaching and writing about living in sync with your hormones, there have been quite a few advancements in research and new books to the market, but Lichterman pioneered this methodology in 1999.

If you feel as if you're having a harder time than most with these hormonal fluctuations, please discuss PMDD with your doctor, and go through the checklist on the IAPMD.org website. In Episode 130 of the *Slow Living* podcast, I interview the founder of this website,

Sandi MacDonald. Premenstrual Dysphoric Disorder (PMDD) is a cyclical, hormone-based mood disorder with symptoms arising during the premenstrual, or luteal, phase of the menstrual cycle and subsiding within a few days of menstruation. It affects an estimated 5.5 percent of women and AFAB individuals of reproductive age. While PMDD is directly connected to the menstrual cycle, it's not a hormone imbalance. PMDD is a severe negative reaction in the brain to the natural rise and fall of estrogen and progesterone.[21]

Perimenopause symptoms can begin as early as your late thirties and can last up to fifteen years for some women before full menopause. If you find that you're struggling with uncomfortable physical, emotional, or psychological issues, please reach out to your doctor to discuss hormone replacement therapy protocols, and whether you may benefit. There is a lot of new research surrounding hormone replacement therapy, so please don't dismiss this without further exploration. A great book to add to your home library is *The Menopause Manifesto* by Dr. Jen Gunter.

# 5. Regular Medical Appointments

This section is fairly self-explanatory. You need to know where you stand. Every year, see a doctor. Twice a year, see a dentist. Oral health directly ties into your overall physical health. Make sure you know that your cholesterol numbers and the rest of your blood panel is up to par.

You've only got this one body.

Treat it right so it will treat you right. And remember: *you are your own best expert.*

The last bit of health advice I'm going to give you is to research and read and then research and read some more.

There is a ton of health advice at your fingertips, for free, on the internet. Use it. Absorb it.

Learn every single thing you possibly can about what works for your own particular body.

## 6. Mental Health

Reams of research have confirmed that your brain and your body are connected, and it's very hard to have good mental health without taking care of your physical health. That said, many people have bodies that don't function the way that they'd like them to, or that aren't as agile or fit as they once were.

That's okay. I'd still like for you to do all that you can to continue on a path toward better physical health. While you do this, you may find that your mental health also improves.

In 2022, the American Foundation for Suicide Prevention published research from the CDC that suicide was the eleventh-leading cause of death among American adults. This same research also found that 94 percent of Americans believe that suicide is preventable.[22]

Please take care of your mental health.

If you're having a difficult time and aren't able to shake intrusive thoughts on your own using the suggestions in this book or in others, reach out to your doctor and ask for help. If you find that your doctor isn't listening or taking your concerns seriously, find another one and don't stop trying until you feel validated and listened to. Thankfully, we live in an era where discussions about mental health are no longer taboo.

Personally, I struggle with insomnia and anxiety and find that in order to best take care of my brain and body I need to follow my own game plan that I've developed through years of tweaking and fine-tuning. I need to spend as much time outside as I can each day, drink a lot of water, get in my 10,000 steps, limit sugar, caffeine, and alcohol, and get at least seven hours of sleep. This list may sound exhausting to some, but I find that I have more energy and my anxiety is kept in check if I consciously decide to regularly prioritize these things.

Your brain and body may function differently than mine does. This is why I would never tell you, or anyone I coach, that this particular list must be followed. We are not living a one-size-fits-all life. Research. Read. Investigate. And be curious as to what foods, drinks, activities, and movement plans work best for you and your life.

When you do this, you'll be using the Mindset + Action + Consistency = Success formula exactly the way that it was designed.

I'm a firm believer that the more you know, the better you are when it comes to your health. Take in as much information as you can, and then filter it. You only have this brain and body for a limited amount of time. You might as well use it the best way you can.

# Chapter 11

# Build a Secure Future: Finances

"Money, like emotions, is something you must
control to keep your life on the right track."
—Natasha Munson

The last piece of the foundational level of the Peace
Pyramid is finances.

In order to live a calm, peaceful life filled with joy,
it's important to take charge of your financial health and
literacy. Gaining control of what's coming in and going out
is beneficial for your everyday well-being.

For many people, talking about money is not a fun topic.
But it's necessary.

There are five things to pay attention to when planning
out your finances:

1. Budgeting
2. Debt (fixing the past)

3. Retirement (FIRE and FIBRE)
4. College (maybe)
5. What does Financial Peace[23] look like to you?

Let's dive into these aspects of finances in more detail.

# 1. Budgeting

If you're anything like me, the word *budget* doesn't sound all that fun. It may remind you of the word *diet*, which we talked about in the last chapter.

It's not a fun word because it conjures images of deprivation and scarcity. You aren't allowed to do this or that because of the evil "budget."

But this is real life and in order to adult up in real life, sometimes you have to do things that might not be classified as fun.

To revisit the whole koala analogy, a koala's diet is eucalyptus leaves. It's not restrictive, it's not controlling, it just happens to be eucalyptus leaves. We can apply this same concept to budgeting. This isn't a restriction. This is knowing what's coming and going at all times.

Most of us get money each and every month. For some, it comes from multiple sources at random times (this is the case for those who are self-employed or whose monthly income fluctuates).

Please shed any preconceived notions or opinions you may have about whether budgets "work for you" or whether or not you "tried that once." You're going to need to make a spending plan.

That's all a budget is—a spending plan.

Back in high school economics class you may have been asked to make a list estimating all of your living expenses.

It's time to do this again, but not as an estimation. You'll need to use actual figures.

This isn't because you're on any sort of restriction, nor should you feel shame about accurately reporting these numbers. You are merely stating the facts so if anything happens to you, another person can swoop in if necessary and figure out what's going on with your finances.

Sometimes people I work with will cut me off when I start talking about making an expenditure plan because they say that their spouse or significant other deals with the finances.

Okay! That's great!

But, now *you* do, too. You need to know where everything is going—if you have a joint bank account and joint expenses, then you need to know everything. If you have to sit down and meet with your spouse so you can understand the bank accounts, then do it.

It's important to be proactive in this part of your life. It's not fair in a partnership for one person to know everything and the other to be in the dark. You wouldn't want a business partnership to be this way, and a marriage is the most important business partnership you're ever going to be involved in.

So, what is included in this spending plan?

Glad you asked! *All* of your monthly expenses need to be listed: home (mortgage/rent), utilities (gas, electric, water), TV (cable, dish, streaming services), gym, daycare/preschool, sports classes for kids, housekeeping, gardening, cell phone, credit cards, school loans, home loans, car payments, groceries, etc.

You also need to have a line for each month for: eating out, household items (toilet paper, cleaning supplies; these aren't groceries—groceries are food!), diapers, healthcare, birthdays, entertainment, holiday expenses, vacation fund, emergency fund, college, and retirement.

Now your goal is to identify each dollar that comes into your household. Most financial advisors (and I agree with this) instruct clients to pay into retirement, investments, and any other savings accounts directly from your paycheck.

In most finance books, this is called "paying yourself first."

This is money you never see. You automatically arrange it the same way you automatically pay into social security and, in most cases, healthcare. This preallocated money comes directly out of your paycheck and goes into your savings accounts.

How much should go into these savings accounts? That's something you (and your spouse, if applicable) need to figure out.

The best rule of thumb is: *the more the better*.

If you find that after paying all of your bills each month you have extra wiggle-room money, then you need to increase your retirement savings. The money you save for retirement is your most important investment, and it's also the very best gift you can give your children.

Let me repeat that: The best gift you can give your children, before a video game console, before a trip to Disney World or a snowboarding adventure or a big college savings account, is to *have your retirement account fully funded*. The gift of not having to worry about you in your retirement is the very best gift you can ever give your children.

It's suggested that you have ready access to enough money for at least six months of living expenses. This can be in a regular savings account or a checking account—but it needs to be "liquid" money that you can get to easily (which means, don't have it tied up in a long-term investment or the stock market, things you can't access immediately, if necessary).

Your emergency fund is just that. It's available in case of an emergency. An emergency isn't a family wedding or a cruise. It's to be used in case of a natural disaster or sudden job loss because of illness or being laid off.

Ideally, you never touch this emergency fund, and you then have this nice pot of money growing interest that you can use if necessary. If you'd like to spend the tiny bit of accumulated interest each year or roll that over into a larger interest-yielding account, then go for it. That's "free" money—and money you deserve to play with since you did such a good job of funding your emergency account.

But let's say that where you are personally struggling is with the actual money allotment—there just isn't enough to go into each slot to pay the line item, or you think you're spending too much in a certain area.

That's understandable, and this is exactly why you need a budget or spending plan to keep you accountable.

Most people overspend in two categories: groceries (food for preparing at home) and entertainment (which includes eating out, weekend activities like concerts, and more). The best way to trim the amount you spend in both areas is to go old school and use cash.

The cash envelope system is not a new idea. Most people have heard about going all cash, and putting each week's spending allotment into an envelope. When the money is gone, it's gone.

So, if most people have *heard* of this, does that mean that most people *do* this?

Not at all.

If I had to guess, I'd say 99.9999999999999999999 percent of all the people who have heard the advice to use cash in preallocated envelopes don't do it.

And then they wonder what they are doing wrong and why they can't get their spending under control.

This is the American Way. We want what we want when we want it.

Even if we can't afford it.

You know this. I know this.

It's a *very easy fix*: if you can't afford it, don't buy it.

I get asked a lot of grocery questions—which is understandable considering I have written quite a few cookbooks and run a recipe website. About once a week, I'm asked what a "normal" grocery budget should be. So here's the thing: we need to remember that the only category that should be purchased from your grocery budget is *food*. Not lightbulbs, not mascara or cat litter—just food.

So let's start at a baseline. The USDA (United States Department of Agriculture) provides four examples of food plans based on different household budgets. These plans—aptly named the "thrifty," "low-cost," "moderate-cost," and "liberal" food plans—provide instructions and specifics regarding which food and beverages can be purchased and prepared so that any household can sustain a healthy diet.[24]

The thrifty food plan serves as the basis for the Supplemental Nutrition Assistance Program (SNAP) maximum benefit allotments. The low-cost, moderate-cost, and liberal food plans are used by various federal and state agencies and the court system to help allocate support payments.

This should be your starting point, and you can find charts that are updated monthly at USDA.gov.

It's useful to know this baseline number because if you're spending a lot more than this on groceries (food only) each month, you might want to reign yourself in.

The best way to do this is to utilize a meal plan. I'm a huge proponent of meal planning because not only does it alleviate decision fatigue, it really is a useful way to keep your monthly food budget in line.

When you begin grocery shopping with a meal plan in place, your grocery budget is going to stretch so much farther than it would if you just randomly walked through the supermarket's aisles throwing random food and household items into the cart.

## 2. Debt (Fixing the Past)

It sounds harsh, but the best way to deal with debt is to never get into it.

But if you're carrying a consumer debt month to month, then you need to get out of it. Outside of paying for your absolute necessities—housing, utilities, food, healthcare, and retirement—you'll need to figure out a plan to ensure that your consumer credit card debt is annihilated.

Debt is an anchor around your neck. It just needs to be dealt with, and you won't feel at peace or in control of your life plan until it's gone.

One of my hobbies is saving money. I don't shop for fun and I prefer to not buy things unless I know I can pay in cash and know the item will work in my life or fit into my closet or home.

That said, when I was in college and a newlywed I did have consumer credit card debt—to the tune of about $35,000.

I remember signing up for credit cards at the tables they had around the school so I could get the "free" gift—which was usually something stupid like a king-size candy bar or a branded frisbee.

I was young and was lured in by the "if you sign up now you can save 15 percent on this purchase" sales pitch.

Thankfully, I only lived this way for about a year and then stopped charging pizza deliveries and McDonald's meals. It's not all that fun to pay interest on your $4.25 cheeseburger meal a few months later!

This debt was knocked out in about a year, and my husband and I used a similar approach to save that same money for a down payment for our first house.

It sort of sounds mind-boggling, but paying down roughly $30,000 and then saving that amount in less than two years really wasn't that big of a deal.

We just did what we had to do.

It was easier then than it would be now, because it was just the two of us and so we just stopped buying things. All of our money went toward paying off debt, and then it went into a savings account.

We canceled cable.

We canceled the cell phones.

We stopped eating out.

We had date nights at the library and rented videos for free.

If we wanted a dinner out, we called our parents and asked if we could come over.

We had plenty of clothes in the closet, so not buying anything for two years wasn't all that big of a deal.

We canceled the annual vacation we used to take with friends, and we even decided to forgo camping for those two years.

Meal planning became part of our norm. I vividly remember counting out frozen corn dogs and only heating one each because the large box needed to last the entire month. It didn't feel like that big of a deal for us because we had a plan in place and were merely following the plan.

We discussed the plan weekly and went over our numbers and were so focused on our goal that we never lost sight or track of what we wanted. All overtime or "extra" money we found here or there went toward the debt, and after that was taken care of, it went into savings.

(I wouldn't recommend this if you're planning to keep your car for the long term, but both of us had old cars and so we stopped paying for upkeep and just ran them into the ground. When our cars died, we traded them in for a bit off of our next used vehicles. The cars were useless and were most certainly used for scrap metal, but we were able to negotiate a pretty good trade-in price for our next purchase nonetheless.)

**"Just because you can buy it doesn't mean that you can afford it."**
**—Suze Orman**

There are two different paths that people take when debt comes up, and by the time they are in their thirties the paths are firmly divided:

1. Make more money
2. Reduce costs

It's up to you which way you want to go, but I'm of the belief that you do both.

I believe in drastically reducing costs by all means. I believe in teaching my kids the difference between a need and a want, and I model this behavior to them.

For instance, I'm not one to prioritize massages and regular manicures. To me, those are not necessities, they are luxuries. For some of my friends, however, these things are needs, and they are perfectly happy to work longer hours or for a few more months to pay for them.

I personally would rather put that money into a retirement account, but it's not my place to begrudge anyone their choices.

This is it. We only have one life to live.

We are all playing the Game of Life here, and it's your choice where you're going to direct your little plastic car.

I can only tell you from my hundreds of hours of working with people from all walks of life that if keeping up with the superficial Joneses is of utmost importance to you, you may never feel the peace that comes from living within your means.

One of my favorite things to remember when you start thinking that the "grass is always greener" is that if you just take the time to water your own grass, it'll green up. Every time.

If you're looking to read more about personal finance, I recommend the book *Simple Path to Wealth* by JL Collins, which outlines a straightforward investment strategy for achieving financial independence through saving, investing, and living below one's means.

## 3. Retirement (FIRE and FIBRE)

There has been a movement for a few decades called FIRE, which stands for **F**inancial **I**ndependence **R**etire **E**arly.

Proponents of FIRE look at time as the most valuable resource of all and propose that the best way to live life is to become financially independent as early as possible and then retire to enjoy the limited amount of time you have (left) on this planet, however you choose.

Knowing what you are working toward (Step 2, calculate your GPS) is a fantastic way to live your life, and it helps to calculate your FIRE number.

A down-and-dirty way of doing so is to take the amount of money you spend each year (not your income, your expenses) and multiply it by twenty-five. If your yearly expenses add up to roughly $60,000, your FIRE number would be $1.5 million.

The traditional recommended withdrawal from retirement savings is 4 percent. If you withdraw 4 percent of your saved $1.5 million each year, that's the $60,000 you need for your living expenses, assuming you're not planning to increase your current annual spending. Knowing this number is an important part of long-term retirement planning and saving and the first step in becoming financially independent.

I like the FIRE mindset and methodology, but I like to throw a "B" in there—to turn the acronym into FIBRE. This now stands for **F**inancial **I**ndependence **B**efore **R**etiring **E**arly.

Many people enjoy their job and the perks and socialization it provides, yet the peace of mind that comes from knowing they could walk away from it once they reach financial freedom is immensely gratifying.

So, take some time and do some math. Figure out your current annual spending, and then calculate what your FIRE number is by multiplying that by twenty-five. How close are you to that number? How many more years do you need to work and save to get to it?

I know that this can be a rather daunting and uncomfortable task for many—it was for me, too. I recommend spending some time taking an honest assessment of your current spending and saving. If you find that you're overwhelmed or are unable to do this assignment, reach out to a financial advisor, debt consolidator, or another trusted mentor for help.

# Minutes Count

I'm not suggesting that having more money wouldn't be wonderful.

I think we can all agree that money is important, and when you've got a bunch of it you probably don't worry about things the way you would if you don't have a bunch of it.

That's not what I mean. What I mean is that you can *always* make another dollar.

But you can't make another minute.

I try not to waste time doing things that aren't important, and I don't want to suggest things for you that aren't immediately helpful for your own day-to-day living and for your own path to peace.

In order to best apply the Mindset + Action + Consistency = Success formula to your personal finances, it's important to recognize that once you have a certain plan laid out to pay off consumer debt and save adequately for the future, you stick with it until you reach the financial goals you've set. It's really easy to begin increasing your spending on nonessential items and luxuries when discretionary income rises. This is known within personal finance communities as "lifestyle creep."

Remember that the very first component of the Peace Pyramid that we discussed was Time Management.

Purposefully decide that you'll figure out what your numbers are, and then revisit them often to ensure that you're on the right path.

The pyramid's three foundational elements—Time Management, Health, and Finances—are paramount to creating a strong, steady, and sustainable life. In fact, these pieces are so important that it would be okay to stay here, within this foundational level, for many years before trying to add to your Peace Pyramid.

# 4. College (Maybe)

If you have children of any age, chances are you're already thinking about college and how you're going to pay for it.

First off, figure out the average cost for a four-year school in your state, and then increase it by about 20 percent.

Many parents decide that they'll pay for in-state tuition and then have their child take out loans or earn scholarships to make up any difference for an out-of-state or private college.

Now remember, these are just ideas, information to help you decide your priorities. And there's no need to worry that you are behind. You can start now to plan and save in a way that works best for you and your family.

You won't be surprised to hear me say that while saving for college for each of your children is a good thing, saving for your retirement is much more important. I emphasized it earlier in this section but it bears repeating: the very best gift you can ever give your children is a solid retirement for you and your spouse (if applicable).

Give your children (or the rest of your family if you don't have children) the gift of not having to worry about you financially.

There are many tools to help your kids get the best education on a limited budget. My favorite resources include two books written by Zac Bissonnette: *Debt-Free U: How I Paid for an Outstanding College Education Without Loans, Scholarships, or Mooching off My Parents* and *How to Be Richer, Smarter, and Better-Looking Than Your Parents*. My own children have read these books, and I've recommended them countless times to friends and coaching clients and discussed them on my podcast.

> "It's not about 'what can I
> accomplish?' but 'what do I want
> to accomplish?' Paradigm shift."
> —Brené Brown

My intention is to get you to think deeply about all this stuff, to really dive deep and understand where each and every dollar you spend goes, and to get a grip on your finances so you know you're on the right path.

Just like G.I. Joe taught in the commercial that ran seemingly nonstop in the 1980s: knowing is half the battle.

There is nothing wrong with a nice vacation to a tropical location, but if you don't have a retirement plan, college savings plan, insurance policy, and an emergency fund in place, an expensive trip won't bring you peace.

Instead, it will only provide a fleeting illusion of peace and tranquility—and a sunburn.

Trust me, the vacation will feel much better and much more relaxing if you have paid for it without debt and know that you truly deserved it, because you planned and saved for it. Not because you got bamboozled into a marketing ploy.

If you find yourself surrounded by social media images and stories of people living in extravagant ways and this is making you feel inadequate, go back to Step 1 of the 5 Steps to Slow Living and declutter. Turn off social media and unsubscribe from marketing emails that make you feel like you're missing out.

## 5. What Does Financial Peace Look Like?

This is a tricky question, because it looks different to each and every person, and it can look different to you from year to year and sometimes even from day to day.

Most advisors believe that true financial peace comes from knowing that you can pay your bills each month and have enough left over to fully fund all of your savings accounts, and then have a tiny bit of wiggle room for frivolity.

I believe that peace comes with planning.

And I believe in planning for frivolity so I never feel deprived.

This is it. This is life. It's a long journey filled with big decisions but many, many more little daily decisions that can try to pull you off course.

These are my parting words of wisdom: Don't blindly bump along the path. Pull out a map, plot your route, and follow the course.

You can do this!

# Chapter 12

# Simplify and Succeed: Organization

"With organization comes empowerment."
—Lynda Peterson

Now let's talk a bit about organization. Many people who reach out to me for the first time struggle with organization and feel that their cluttered home is what's keeping them from making forward progress in their lives.

There is a reason that I don't start with organization or try to spend a lot of time uncovering why someone has what they deem a "cluttered home." There are plenty of very successful people who don't have super-organized living spaces, offices, or desks.

Organization and order are lovely and can help you to feel productive, but they aren't a marker of a life well-lived. Instead, the first few sections of the Peace Pyramid—Time Management, Health, and Finances—build up the base to create a strong and stable foundation for your dream life.

I would really like to stress that if those components aren't in place, if you are neglecting your health, or if you don't have a plan to deal with your finances, please go back and get those things in order.

Because having an organized linen closet is *not a necessity* in life; it's a nicety. But your health? Your future retirement? Those are imperative.

If you have been a user of my *Totally Together: Shortcuts to an Organized Life* planner, a lot of this is going to sound familiar, and that's because the basics of household and life organization are the same as the groundwork laid out in my planner.

We are going to discuss The Daily 7—which are the daily chores that need to occur each and every day, rain or shine.

Then we will do a brief recap of the PROM method of organization—purge, remove, organize, and maintain—which we discussed earlier in the first step of Slow Living in Part 2, Chapter 4. Finally, I'll lay out a timeline to get everything done around the house on a weekly, monthly, and seasonal basis.

## The Daily 7 for a Highly Successful Household

I believe that seven key chores need to be accomplished daily to keep your home running smoothly and to promote tranquility. These tasks can be done by anyone in the family. Feel free to delegate to your spouse and children. This is the *family's* home, and these are the *family's* chores.

## 1. Make Beds Right Away

As soon as you rise in the morning, make your bed. Help or remind children to do the same. This is a wonderful habit to get into. The sense of accomplishment that comes from seeing a made bed is enough to carry many people through the entire morning. "It's only 6:30 a.m. and I've already *done* something!"

## 2. Do One Complete Load of Laundry

A complete load of laundry is washed, dried, folded, and put away. The methodology from my book *Clean Less, Play More* is if you don't have to wash it, don't. If you don't have to separate colors, don't. Assign each household member a bath towel to use for an entire week. Unless you have severe allergies, change linens only when needed (I change our sheets every two to three weeks unless someone is sick or has an accident).

## 3. Empty All Garbage Cans

Empty all wastebaskets and garbage cans at least once a day. If you have stinky items (such as diapers or tuna fish cans), take them to the outside trash bin. Trust me, you'll be a much happier camper in the morning if last night's chicken bones were taken all the way outside and not allowed to stink up the house overnight. Make sure the recyclables are also taken out.

## 4. Keep Your Kitchen Sink Empty

The fourth habit to include in your daily routine is to keep your kitchen sink empty. This means that when you finish using a plate or utensil, either put the item directly into the dishwasher or wash it by hand. If dishes are allowed to rest in the sink, other pieces of flatware are mysteriously attracted by some unseen magnetic force and all of a sudden the sink is completely overrun and rendered useless. Also, there are very few things as discouraging as waking up in the morning to last night's dirty dishes.

## 5. Clean Up After Yourself, and Help Children Do the Same

I still have just as much trouble with this one as my kids do. I regularly forget to return the scissors to the kitchen drawer, or I leave a magazine in the middle of the living room floor. I'm getting better, which annoys my children, because there is nothing better than catching Mom doing something "wrong." Anyhow—a great rule to follow is, if you get it out, put it away. If you see it, pick it up. Don't ignore the Cheerio under the kitchen table; pick it up before it gets stepped on and crumbs are spread throughout the house.

I'm not suggesting you police yourself or your children nonstop. Nobody likes to be nagged, and you don't need to feel as if you must constantly stand guard. If you're home throughout the day, stage cleanups at natural stopping points, such as before snack and lunch time, and encourage children to clean up one activity before beginning another.

One of my favorite mom friends helped her children learn this valuable skill by keeping the puzzles and games out of reach. If her children wanted a new item, they needed to "hand in" the previous one.

## 6. Wipe Down the Bathroom

Once a day, quickly wipe down all surfaces in each bathroom. A good time to do this is after a bath or shower, when there are still water puddles. Grab an item from the dirty clothes pile (T-shirts work great) and use it to quickly dry the shower doors or ledges of the tub. This will help keep the majority of mold and soap scum from adhering. Many people leave a squeegee in the shower to use on the glass door. You can then use the damp clothing item to wipe up the floor and around the base of the sink and around the toilet.

Keep a package of disinfecting wipes in each bathroom. At some point throughout the day, take a few seconds to quickly wipe down the toilet, inside and out.

I began this system of quick bathroom wipe-downs when my children were toddlers and I needed to stay in the bathroom with them while they bathed. Regardless of how careful they were not to splash, water got onto the floor. Since the floor was already wet, I used the dirty towel to do the quick mop-down and used the time they were in the bath to wipe down the sink and toilet.

## 7. 10-Minute Tidy Before Bed

It's amazing how much can be accomplished when you (and your children) are trying to beat the clock. Put this competitive nature to good use by setting a timer each night and instilling a 10-Minute Tidy cleaning time for the family. Have everybody run through the house as quickly as possible looking for stray shoes, toys, art supplies, etc. This is not the time to color-coordinate the stuffed animals—just do a quick run through the whole house.

If you have had an exceptionally busy day, the 10-Minute Tidy is the one assignment you shouldn't miss.

We have five people in our family. Since there are five of us, when I set that microwave timer each night at about 7:30, we actually can get fifty minutes of tidying done. That's a pretty big deal!

For me, I want the front room and the kitchen table cleaned up—completely clear. I don't want to see backpacks by the front door spilling contents, and I'd like the shoes put all the way into the closet and the jackets hung on hooks.

This literally takes about fifteen seconds, but the peace of mind it gives me to not have a cluttered front entry in the morning is HUGE.

If this list of seven tasks is too daunting, start with the 10-Minute Tidy each evening before bed.

You can DO THIS.

## Everyday and Seasonal PROMing

The next big part of organization is PROM (remember: **P**urge, **R**emove, **O**rganize, **M**aintain). We discussed this earlier in the 5 Steps to Slow Living. This is a great way to simplify your day-to-day life, and it also is a fantastic way to rid your home of no longer needed or wanted items.

Seriously. It's that easy, and quite honestly, *very* therapeutic. Mental health experts agree that clutter and visual chaos can raise anxiety and cortisol levels in some people.[25] When there are too many things to look at, your brain will automatically begin sorting the items, which sends a signal that there is work to do—this can be quite daunting if you're returning home from a tiring day at work only to be bombarded with even more to do!

After you have maintained The Daily 7 for a few weeks, it's time to take stock of junk lurking in your home. You really don't need eight years' worth of *Home Beautiful* magazines, do you? Do you really need the torn jeans you haven't worn since you were sixteen? How about the electric bills from 1993? And for goodness' sake, get rid of the old letters from that cute guy in high school science class. You don't need them anymore.

I'll let you in on a little secret: If your kids don't play with their toys, it's not because they don't have enough to play with. It's because they have *too much*, and they don't even know what they have anymore. Start purging.

Now, here's what *not* to do.

Don't go room by room right now and start emptying dresser drawers and pulling things out of your kitchen cabinets.

Don't start a project that you can't finish by the end of the day.

You need to be able to go to bed feeling accomplished and relaxed—not overwhelmed because you just dumped twelve years' worth of accumulated clutter onto the floor of the living room.

Remember, the key to this step of your pyramid is ORGANIZATION. Let's be organized with how you tackle your PROMing. You can't expect your house to look like a magazine or design catalog, but you can expect children (and spouses!) to clean up after themselves.

I like to approach maintenance PROMing on a seasonal calendar.

| Spring | Summer | Fall | Winter |
|--------|--------|------|--------|
| kids' dresser drawers, toys/playroom<br><br>master bedroom drawers, closet | garage, backyard, toolshed, etc.<br><br>office/desk<br><br>filing cabinets, etc. | kitchen, dining room, linen closet | living room, super quick once-over again of kids' dresser drawers/closet and the master bedroom drawers/closet |

After a while, the annual purge of each section of your house is going to take less than twenty minutes—it really just becomes second nature and feels more natural the more you do it.

> "Everyone can do simple things to make a difference, and every little bit does count."
> —Stella McCartney

What about all the dirt and grime you're worried about? What about dusting and vacuuming and mopping and scrubbing toilets? Am I trying to tell you that all you have to do is The Daily 7 and PROM here and there and you'll never need to scrub another toilet?

No. Not really. But also, YES.

The thing is—you're going to find that a super quick vacuum or sweep once a week and a capful of bleach in the toilet bowls weekly is all it's really going to take, once you get the hang of The Daily 7.

Why is that? It's because at the end of the day when you see the crumbs under the kitchen table or the tracked-in mud by the front door, you're going to get a damp towel or disinfecting wipe and clean it up right then and there.

No need to pull out a bucket and mop. Just squat down and take care of it (also, this raises your NEAT, as discussed within the Health section!).

Don't make housework harder or more involved than it needs to be.

This isn't a restaurant that needs to be sterilized each and every day. It's your home. And you are in charge.

Also, if you simply leave your shoes by the front door and don't walk throughout the house in them, you will automatically have MUCH cleaner floors!

# A Recipe for Success

Let's do a tiny recap. All you need to do to have a truly clean and organized home is:

1.  Do The Daily 7.
2.  Once a week do the big guns like Sweep, Dust, Vacuum, Mop.
3.  And then PROM on a seasonal basis.

This may seem simple, but I urge you to try it for a quarter and see if you feel like things start to fall into place.

Now let's talk about house cleaners. I'm going to be uber-blunt: many people who utilize house cleaners fall into one or both of the following categories:

1.  They don't have as much disposable income as they think they do (see Finance section).
2.  They aren't as organized and tidy as they think they are.

Having a housekeeper come in to do the windows and the blinds and to tackle the floors in a really detailed way is lovely, but it's a lot like taking your car to the dealership to get detailed.

It's a nicety. Not a necessity.

A necessity is to take the McDonald's wrappers out of your car so it doesn't smell like a French fry factory.

But having someone go over your car with toothpicks and Q-tips and Armor All the dashboard? This is not a necessity. It's a nicety. A luxury.

If you have followed the steps in Chapter 11 and have created a budget that includes housekeeping on a regular basis, that's great—I'm not trying to take away your housekeepers!

But let's remember what your goals are here. Your goals are most likely to include being happy, healthy, safe, and secure, and feeling at peace. Your goal is to fall asleep each night knowing you've done your very best and that your children are being brought up knowing what an honest day's work looks like and how to, someday, be a full-fledged grown-up.

A self-sufficient grown-up.

If your children grow up never having to change their bedsheets or push a vacuum, what have you taught them? To expect someone else will do it for them? That it's okay to simply place dishes in the sink and not worry about it because the cleaner will take care of it?

Is that what you'd like for your children?

To be *above* housework? To be better than making a bed or washing a dish?

No. I didn't think so.

The very best thing you can do is to clean up after yourself on a day-to-day basis and expect your children to do the same.

Now, again, if you have room in your monthly budget for housekeeping after properly saving for a rainy day and retirement, great. Utilize a housekeeping service.

## Working with Your Kids

We just touched on this, but let's go into a bit more detail. Regardless of whether you have outside help in cleaning your home, your children still need to learn to put away their toys, hang up their backpacks, make their beds, and contribute to the general upkeep of the home. Not only does this teach them the importance of being a team player, but it also encourages self-sufficiency.

The following chart breaks down developmentally appropriate chores for children of all ages:

| 1–2 years | 3–6 years | 7–10 years | Preteen–young adult |
|---|---|---|---|
| Babies and young children enjoy being "big helpers," and can begin to participate in the following household chores with adult supervision, help, and guidance: | Preschool-age children can continue to help with all of the chores previously listed, along with the following added responsibilities: | School-age children are capable of fulfilling all of the tasks previously listed, as well as these new additions: | Although teenagers would rather lie around and text all day, they are fully capable to help with most of the housekeeping duties, inside and out, including these new ones: |
| – sort laundry | – make their own beds | – complete an entire load of wash | – vacuum the house |
| – empty wastebaskets | – load and unload the dishwasher with assistance | – help younger siblings put away laundry | – sweep the house |
| – bring in the mail/ newspaper | – help younger siblings clean up strewn toys | – vacuum their own rooms | – clean the refrigerator |
| – match socks | | – maintain order in their bedrooms | – wipe down the bathrooms |
| – pull up bed clothes | – feed and water pets | – sweep the kitchen | – wipe down the kitchen countertops |
| – empty spoons and plasticware from the dishwasher caddy | – pull weeds<br>– water plants | – load and unload the dishwasher independently | |

| 1–2 years | 3–6 years | 7–10 years | Preteen–young adult |
|---|---|---|---|
| – put toys away in appropriate containers<br><br>– "dust and clean" with a baby wipe | – use a whisk broom to clean up crumbs under the dinner table<br><br>– use a handheld vacuum cleaner to spot-clean, or to vacuum the stairs<br><br>– put away their own laundry<br><br>– set the table for meals | – walk the dog<br><br>– clear the table after meals | – help younger siblings as needed<br><br>– perform more strenuous work in the garden |

This may seem like a lot, but remember that back in the "olden days," children were expected to be productive members of the household. Whenever I start to feel "mean," I think of *The Long Winter* by Laura Ingalls Wilder and remember all that the girls did to help Pa and Ma.

I also think of my friend Alison, who homeschooled her nine children. Alison once told me that a parent's job was to raise *adults*, not children. By the time children leave for college, they should be able to make a meal, sew on a button, do laundry, mow the lawn, and (in their household) milk a goat.

Don't expect your children to instantly adhere to a list of chores without instruction, direction, and diligent guidance. Remember the old adage "monkey see, monkey do"—lead by example and set regular 10-Minute Tidies into your household routine to help keep your home picked up and put together.

## Inherited Items

Many people decide to reach out for help with organizing and decluttering when they inherit items from a deceased family member.

Sentimental items are the most difficult of all to PROM, and my best suggestion would be to go as slowly as you can so you can process your grief and memories before haphazardly discarding cherished items that may very well be irreplaceable.

If you have the ability to do so, consider holding off decluttering sentimental items until you have processed your grief from losing your loved one. This way you can look at the items as *things* and not as extensions of the person.

This may take some time, and I urge you to give yourself patience and grace. There is no right or wrong way to process grief, and rushing the process or beating yourself up for not doing it "correctly" won't help.

Janelle Azar is a professional organizer who recorded episode 101 of the *Slow Living* podcast with me. We discussed Sentimental Decluttering, and she suggested envisioning where inherited items will be housed, used, and displayed before agreeing to keep them.

Do not take things into your home that don't serve your needs or provide cherished memories. Often guilt is cited as the reason for keeping inherited items, but

I counsel clients that keeping things out of obligation, and not out of usefulness or fondness, isn't a great way to keep memories alive.

Tastes and styles change from generation to generation, and it isn't practical to think that you'll keep certain pieces of furniture or personal items indefinitely.

Take time to process your guilt and uncomfortable feelings and make peace with them before moving forward with the **PROM** technique.

If we apply the Mindset + Action + Consistency = Success formula to your organization or decluttering project it might look a little like this:

Mindset: *What am I trying to achieve here? How do I want this space to feel?*

Action: *Implement The Daily 7 and PROM technique as explained fully within this chapter.*

Consistency: *Stick with The Daily 7 indefinitely. If you're in a time pinch or in a particularly busy season of life and only have time to do one out of the seven, choose a 10-Minute Tidy.*

# Chapter 13

# Connect with Purpose: Relationships

"The truth is, some relationships are supposed to last forever, and some are only supposed to last a few days. That's the way life is."
—Sophie Kinsella

In this chapter, we will go over the different relationships in your life, and how to best cultivate each one, because they are all unique in their own ways.

I have purposefully placed relationships as the second-to-last component of the Peace Pyramid. In order to bring variables into your life you cannot fully control (other humans), it's important to feel stable with who you are and with conviction.

Remember, *you* are in charge of you, and we are only going to discuss what part you play in all of your various relationships. You can't change anyone, nor should you try to. If you feel as if you're having issues with relationships in your life and you can't seem to connect in a way that works, it may be helpful to get outside help.

You can't expect other people to change or become "better" or more forgiving or more helpful. You can only change your own actions and expectations. It's not fun to feel as if all the people and acquaintances in your life are out to get you. If this is the case, please seek help from a trained professional.

Now let's break it down into five major categories of relationships and take a closer look at each one.

## The Five Key Relationships

1.   Yourself
2.   Spouse, Significant Other, Partner
3.   Your Children
4.   Parents and Siblings
5.   Friends and Coworkers

### 1. Yourself

The very first relationship you need to cultivate is with yourself. This is a big one, and there are tons of resources and courses available just for this one segment. But the fact is, you can't have a proper relationship with anyone if you don't know who you are as a person and what makes you tick.

Taking the time to get to know *you*, and your deepest, most innermost thoughts, is one of the most beneficial gifts you can ever give to yourself, not to mention your spouse, your children, and the rest of the important people in your life.

The good news is that if you take the time to go through the 5 Steps to Slow Living in each area of the Peace Pyramid, you have already done much of the heavy lifting. And that's fantastic news!

## Introverted Versus Extroverted

There are many different personality tests and quizzes you can find online to help you uncover your personality type. You may have a lot of fun going down the rabbit hole of discovering your Myers–Briggs characteristics, your Enneagram type, your human design makeup, and whether you match the qualities revealed according to your astrological sign. These tools are fun and can be useful, but they don't fully define you.

Many psychologists agree that paying attention to how you get your energy and recharge yourself when feeling depleted and discouraged is quite important. Over the years, I've put together some questions to differentiate between *introvert* and *extrovert*. So as a bit of a shortcut, here's a simplified questionnaire to help you get at your basic personality type:

| 1) | Do you feel charged and energized after spending time alone? | Yes / No |
|---|---|---|
| 2) | Do you look forward to attending parties and social gatherings? | Yes / No |
| 3) | Do you tend to keep your thoughts to yourself in meetings and not speak up unless called upon? | Yes / No |
| 4) | Do you prefer to spend free time working on solo hobbies such as reading, gardening, or crafting? | Yes / No |

| 5) | Do you feel comfortable and at ease making small talk with strangers? | Yes / No |
|---|---|---|
| 6) | Do you find you need to take breaks or step away from social situations to recharge during busy events? | Yes / No |
| 7) | Are you comfortable expressing your thoughts and emotions openly, even to people you've just met? | Yes / No |
| 8) | Do you prefer to have a small circle of close friends versus a large circle of acquaintances? | Yes / No |
| 9) | Do you find that you have your best thoughts when you have time to reflect on your own, away from external distractions? | Yes / No |
| 10) | Do you seek out opportunities to meet new people and have social interaction? | Yes / No |

Interpretation:

- Count the number of "Yes" and "No" responses.
- More "Yes" answers suggest a higher likelihood of introversion.
- More "No" answers suggest a higher likelihood of extroversion.
- Remember that introversion and extroversion exist on a spectrum, and some people might exhibit traits of both.

Why is this important? Why does it matter if you are an introvert or an extrovert when it comes to having Peace in your life?

It's because everything we've learned so far is tied directly into who you are as a person. If you're an introvert and you keep joining gyms or exercise groups and then fail miserably, it's not because you stink at exercising or goal keeping. It's because you are going directly against your nature.

By contrast, an extroverted person *loves* going to yoga or spin class. She loves seeing her friends and enjoys the camaraderie.

I happen to be introverted. The way I recharge at the end of the day is to retreat to my own home and go within. That's why I've never been all that good at sticking with a group exercise or yoga class. I will go to classes here and there, but prefer to remain anonymous and just do my own thing.

I go to exercise to help my brain and body, not to socialize.

Once I stopped thinking I was wrong for realizing this about myself, my fitness level took off. I stopped trying to cram my square introverted peg into a round hole of a group exercise class.

So, for me, this means walking, jogging, and rolling out the yoga mat at home.

Sometimes I'll play tennis or go for a long walk with a friend; I love those kinds of things. But I don't have a mindset of working out; I have a mindset of being friendly and cheerful, two distinctly different ideas.

This is very helpful to keep in mind as you navigate through the different relationships you have in your life, especially with those you are the closest to—your significant other and your children.

If your partner comes home from work and you immediately pounce on him because you're an extroverted person and he isn't, and then he's crabby and then you get crabby and then and then . . . See how just knowing how others tick can be immensely beneficial for all of your relationships?

## 2. Your Spouse, Significant Other, Partner

The next-most important relationship in your life is the one you have with your spouse, significant other, or partner. This is your number one confidant and your emotional support person, one with whom you can let your guard down and truly be yourself—flaws and all.

This advice and plan for keeping this particular relationship in your life healthy and secure will work regardless of your marital status. Whomever you choose to spend your life with will also benefit from these suggestions!

When it comes down to it, the key is *communication*.

We've all heard it. We all know it. Communication and open dialogue are the very most important pieces of a healthy relationship and the cornerstone of all high-functioning marriages or partnerships.

If you don't feel like you have a good path of communication with your spouse, if you feel like you can't truly be yourself and vice versa, this is a red flag.

That said, there is more than one way to have a happy and healthy marriage. I'm not here to preach to you about how to have the perfect marriage.

There's no such thing.

Life is just too long and too uncertain to have black-and-white absolutes.

Some people say that you can't ever go to bed angry if you want a happy marriage. Some say that you absolutely must have a date night each and every week or your marriage is doomed. Others say that you have to sleep in the same bed every night no matter what, or your marriage isn't going to last. That's ridiculous. What about couples who work opposite shifts? What about chronic insomniacs or snorers?

Marriage is hard work. A relationship with anyone is hard work.

Only *you* know if your marriage is working, and only you know whether you need to tweak something if it's headed toward being broken.

Go Slow. Look within and do some journaling.

## 3. Your Children

It's no wonder our local library and neighborhood bookstore have aisles of books dedicated to parenting and the parent-child relationship. I've been a parent for over twenty years, and I'm still learning new things every day.

I suggest reading a wide array of material and advice and filtering it through your own lens of how you'd like your relationship to be with your children.

In the US, there are two studies that are widely accepted and are what the American Academy of Pediatrics advice is based upon and what is taught within Early Childhood Education classes and handbooks, The Grant Study at Harvard, and the Bowlby & Ainsworth Attachment Theory.

In 1938, Harvard University launched The Grant Study that tracked 268 male Harvard students over seventy years.[26] Their physical and emotional health were recorded, and their successes, or the lack of them, were analyzed.

Researchers arrived at one clear conclusion: Strong relationships are the secret to a happy and successful life. A childhood in which one feels accepted and nurtured is one of the best predictors of adult success, well-being, *and life satisfaction.*

Bowlby & Ainsworth formulated the Attachment Theory in the 1950s, stating that a child who receives warm and nurturing care from a caregiver can develop a secure attachment. A child with a secure attachment is much more likely to have positive development and outcomes.[27]

For you, as a parent, this means that when your children are babies and quite small, be as attentive and present as you can be to help solidify a strong attachment. As your children grow, they will naturally begin to form attachments to other people and become more self-sufficient.

If you find that you're having a hard time self-regulating your emotions while your children are young and aren't able to fully attend to their needs, please seek help. Parenting comes naturally to some, but not all. This is okay, because learning how to best care for a young child is a learnable skill and not something to feel ashamed about.

As your children become more independent, you'll need to adapt and allow the space for growth as they figure out who they are becoming as a person. Again, if you're struggling with allowing this natural life progression to unfold, please seek help from a trusted friend or therapist.

## 4. Parents and Siblings

Just as you'd expect your own children to grow and develop their own personalities, likes, dislikes, and opinions, you will change and evolve as you go through life. This can be tricky if your own parents and siblings don't honor your growth and expansion and expect you to stay the same as you were when you last lived in your childhood home.

Infants and young children are completely dependent on their parents and older siblings to care for all their needs. Through adolescence, they naturally separate from this dependency as they become increasingly interested in developing their own interests, activities, and opinions that may differ from those learned within the family home. If this healthy separation is met with too much resistance, you may find yourself burdened, distressed, or curtailed in your own personal growth. On top of that, you may feel tremendous guilt for feeling this way.

Lindsay C. Gibson, PsyD, in her book *Adult Children of Emotionally Immature Parents: How to Heal from Distant, Rejecting, or Self-Involved Parents*, writes that a child's (even an adult child's) individuality is seen as a threat to an emotionally insecure and immature parent because it stirs up fears about possible rejection or abandonment.[28] If you feel as if you cannot become the adult you'd like to be because your parents or siblings will feel left behind, please explore these thoughts with a therapist.

Remember that you can't change anyone else, only yourself. There are many tools to help navigate sticky family relationships that will keep you moving forward toward your goals and future vision while still maintaining healthy relationships with those who raised you.

## 5. Friends and Coworkers

You also can't expect every relationship you have to last forever. This is key when it comes to your friendships.

There's a rather sappy saying that sometimes you have friends for a "reason" and other times you have them for a "season."

That's okay—people ebb and flow out of your life; you can't expect to hold on to them forever. If you are in college, or newly pregnant, you're certain to resonate quickly with other people in that stage of life.

But many times when graduation day comes or the baby is born, you drift away, and that's nobody's fault. It just means that the relationship has run its course.

Perhaps you exchange emails or holiday cards here or there but it's just not practical to think that the woman you met at your mommy-and-me swim class when you both had young toddlers is going to be a lifelong friend.

Sometimes it works out that way, which is fantastic, but don't go into a friendship believing that every new interaction will be your new best friend.

This comes up quite often when I'm on a coaching call with a newly retired person. Many of us get a lot of our social interaction through the workplace. But the same way I cautioned in the first section of the book that you can't expect your job to provide your identity, you cannot expect your coworkers to be lifelong friends. For most of us, we interact with the people in our office because we are paid to do so.

Yes, you may click with a few coworkers and find that you enjoy each other's company outside of the workplace setting, but you'll need to cultivate those relationships and not expect them to continue without effort.

> "Friendship takes time and energy . . .
> You can luck into something great, but
> it doesn't last if you don't give it proper
> appreciation. Friendship can be so
> comfortable, but don't take it for granted."
> —Betty White

## How to Be a Friend

Now that we've covered the five key categories of relationships, it's a good time to pause and acknowledge that making and maintaining adult friendships is *tough*. Life is full of twists and turns and complications. Here are a few suggestions for maintaining and nurturing friendships.

First, remember that the first step in the 5 Steps to Slow Living is to declutter. Apply this to your friendships—try to cull the negative people in your life. Spending your precious time with people who make you feel bad about yourself or who have a hard time seeing the good in things is not a positive experience for your mental and emotional health.

We've all been around a person who seems to suck the happiness out of a room. Make sure you are not that person, and then begin to walk away from people who don't nurture the person you truly want to be.

**"There comes a time when you have to stop crossing oceans for people who wouldn't jump puddles for you."**
**—J. L. Sheppard**

Second, stop judging without knowing. When you meet someone new, don't immediately assume that you know her story. Because of our human ability to make connections quickly, sometimes we jump to conclusions and size up new people based on past experiences. This is good in some situations; it keeps us out of trouble when we come across a bear in the woods.

But when it comes to meeting new people, this is stereotyping.

Just because you had a bad interaction once with a Mercedes-driving, maroon-haired woman does *not* mean that all women who dye their hair maroon and drive a Mercedes are untrustworthy.

Third, be yourself.

My friend Carla Birnberg, author of *What You Can, When You Can,* wrote on her blog that no matter what, she is "unapologetically herself."[29] It's quite tempting to become chameleon-like in group settings. How many times have you found yourself walking into a party with all the intentions in the world of sticking to your eating plan and having only one glass of wine, but then you let your surroundings get the best of you and suddenly you're face down in the dip bowl?

Yeah, me too.

The thing is that when you aren't confident in who you are and what you want in life, you are more susceptible to peer pressure (and yes, there is definitely such a thing as adult peer pressure!) and following the herd.

It's much easier to smile and nod and go along with the group of PTA ladies who think that the Spell-A-Thon money should be spent on a new smart board even though you think the money should be spent on new outdoor equipment so the kids are up and active instead of sitting and staring at technology all day.

It's a challenge to stand out, I know.

But when you adapt your beliefs and ideas to simply blend in with the group, it can be utterly exhausting to constantly hold your true self back. Be kind, be courteous, but be *you.*

# The Importance of Emotional Support

Magda was a coaching client who was working on finding more friends after a cross-country move. She felt she was missing out because she didn't have a "best friend" as depicted in the movies or on TV. I like to call this the "I want a Gayle syndrome."

Gayle King is Oprah Winfrey's best friend. When Oprah had her daily talk show, Gayle was on the show many times, and they were often showcased on "wild adventures" or doing (what appeared to be) really fun things together. It was also shared that Oprah confided everything in Gayle, and vice versa.

You don't necessarily need a Gayle, though. If you don't have a "best friend" but you have other people in your life that you can be fully yourself around and confide in, you already have an emotional support person. For many of us, this is our spouse or significant other. So, if you've been feeling "less than" about not having a "best friend," please release yourself from thinking there is something wrong. If your emotional needs are being met, you're good!

Please note that it's not appropriate to treat your child as an emotional support person. We discussed in the Finance chapter that the very best gift you can give your child(ren) is the freedom to not worry about your financial well-being. The same could be said of your emotional well-being. If you're having a trying time in your life or marriage or career or something else, or feel as if your emotional needs aren't being fully met, it's wise to seek outside counsel from someone who is not your offspring.

Now let's look at a few more keys to healthy relationships, along with some caution to apply as you navigate them.

# Healing

Many people believe that in order to move forward in life and in their journey toward personal development and personal peace, they need to heal the past completely.

This is a very valid point, and understanding your feelings about a certain relationship in your life and owning those feelings is important work to do.

But in order to move on and heal the past, you don't need to dig up every friend and relative that you got into an argument with at some point and hash it out. That's not productive.

If you are holding on to something from your past which is keeping you from moving forward, then pay attention to that. Take a day or two and really dive deep into your feelings. Maybe write a letter that you don't intend to send. You should absolutely acknowledge the different layers of guilt, remorse, anger, resentment, and hurt that you feel.

But you don't need to confront anyone in order to move on.

It's okay to simply decide to flip a mental switch and leave the past in the past.

Healing comes from within, and you can't move forward if you're hanging on to the past. If you find that this is something you can't do on your own, please reach out to a therapist for help.

## Unconditional Love

This should be a no-brainer for most of us when it comes to our parents, our spouses, or our children, but unfortunately sometimes how we show our love or act toward those who mean the most can be, or appear to be, rather fickle.

And that's not right.

You can't change anyone. If you truly love a person, you love *all* of that person. Even if they aren't a mind reader who you secretly wanted to stop and pick up

Chinese food and a chilled bottle of white wine on the way home from work.

## Unsolicited Advice

My friend Jenny used to call this "assvice"—because it's advice pulled from your (you-know-where).

Guarding against giving (or receiving) unsolicited advice can be really difficult when you're on a path of self-discovery and personal development. It's hard to keep your mouth shut when you see a loved one making mistakes or choices that you know, from experience, are wrong or are more difficult than needed.

My suggestion: hold your tongue unless asked for your opinion, help, or advice.

If you feel awesome on your new sugar-free diet and you can't understand why your friend would poison herself each morning by putting sugar in her coffee and you want to tell her about it? Guess what. *You* are who is at fault. Not your coffee-with-sugar-drinking friend.

This also goes both ways, and for me personally, this came up often with some of my friends and family members when I first started my online business and began writing books.

If you're looking for advice or for a personal mentor, look to someone who has already walked the walk, and simply ignore well-meaning, but not relevant, advice.

## Keep Your Eyes on Your Own Work

If you have a reputation for being someone who engages in gossip, it's time to outgrow this trait. Some people never leave the playground of their childhood, it seems.

"Debate thy cause with thy neighbor
himself; and discover not a secret to
another: Lest he that heareth it put thee to
shame, and thine infamy turn not away."
—Proverbs 25:9–10, KJV

Confident people don't need to feel superior to others. The next time you get together with your friends for brunch and the conversation turns to gossiping about an acquaintance's pending divorce or credit card struggles, remember that what goes around comes around.

Be a good role model. Don't engage in gossip, don't spread it, and don't interact with it online in chat groups. Even if you think you're anonymous (there's a good chance you're not), there is just so much more you could be doing with your time and energy than thinking of ways to tear another person down.

Gossip can sometimes seem like a competitive sport. Before you log into TMZ or pick up the *National Enquirer*, remember that celebrities are still human beings who hurt. Don't contribute to the hurt; rise above it.

TIP: If you're attending a party or gathering, scan the headlines on the Good News Network (goodnewsnetwork. org) and arrive ready to share positive, upbeat current events. It's fun to watch a fun tidbit spread throughout a party, and you can leave knowing that you left positive vibes in your wake.

## Dealing with Negative People

We all have to deal with difficult people at some point, but what can be the most challenging is learning how to deal with negative energy from one of our closest family members or a workmate you simply can't walk away from.

At times, it may not be easy to achieve a balance between a sense of compassion without being dragged into their negativity, which is why I'd like to share with you five simple tips for dealing with a negative family member.

## 1. Accept Them for Who They Are

It may not be easy to offer compassion to someone you feel resentment toward, but trying to understand their feelings, and ultimately accepting them for who they are, will help you feel better when you're around them.

## 2. Create Positive Boundaries

Make sure you're giving them enough space and that you set your own boundaries by staying positive or neutral. Visualizing a protective energy around yourself will also help you feel stronger if you can't put physical distance between you and your family member.

## 3. Be Aware of Your Need to Control

You can't control other people's negativity or opinions, so resist the urge to argue if your family member triggers negative energy inside of you. Your job is not to fix everyone's problems, so instead of being a part of the problem by feeding it with more emotions, disengage by remaining calm and letting yourself be a witness, not a participant.

## 4. Learn from Them

There's always something to learn from any situation, and negative family members can be great spiritual teachers; they can help to show you what you're holding on to. So don't waste the opportunity to learn from these situations.

## 5. Nurture Yourself

This may be the most important tip of all. Remember that by nurturing yourself and your self-confidence, *you* will become stronger!

Tap into your compassion to find inner peace and don't forget to foster the relationships that lift you up and bring you the most happiness!

If we apply the Mindset + Action + Consistency = Success formula to the relationships in your life, it might look a little like this:

Mindset: *Who are the important people in my life? How do I want each of these relationships to function and feel?*

Action: *Decide how often you'd like to communicate with each person, how you'd like to communicate, and then begin adding regular touchpoints to your calendar and/or schedule.*

Consistency: *Nurturing relationships takes time and energy. Regularly evaluate whether your current relationships are contributing to your overall well-being and sense of fulfillment.*

\* \* \*

# You've Reached the Tip of the Pyramid—Peace

You're at the tip of the pyramid! The peak of the mountain! For many, this is where they *start* and then they wonder why they aren't making any traction, and that's why we started at the very bottom. Meditating, daydreaming, and journaling sound great in theory, but you need to have concrete action steps and a well-thought-out plan in order to achieve anything monumental.

That's what we're doing here. We are being monumental.

In order to feel at peace, truly at peace, you need to know who you are, what you stand for, and what your true purpose is.

This is heavy. I caution you to not go too crazy here thinking you need to be the next Dalai Lama or the CEO of a billion-dollar tech start-up. You don't need to be famous or on TV or a household name in order to have purpose in your life.

Throughout your life, your purpose will ebb and flow. Who you are, what you stand for, and what your true purpose is today might not be the same thing you're doing twenty years from now, or even in the next six months.

For me, I'm a natural caretaker. I feel the most fulfilled when I am taking care of others. I like helping people.

I started out caring for animals at a very young age. My parents, thankfully, were quite supportive and allowed me to set up habitats and care for the random worms, caterpillars, and lizards I brought home. As I grew up, this expanded into surprising my parents with pet mice, rats, a bunny, and a few kittens throughout the years.

I remember when I was quite young—maybe only five or six—I had a family of super balls. I built my super ball family an elaborate house in a discarded cardboard box, complete with room dividers built out of folded pieces of construction paper. I talked to my super ball family, made beds for them out of Kleenex, and took them outside for "exercise" (this meant bouncing them).

I was a bit of an odd child . . . but it's who I was, and am, deep down inside. I now feel as if I am living the life I always imagined I would as a little girl. I help people and care for them all day long.

What about you? Are you, at your core, a builder? A creator? Do you lose track of time and feel most in your element when you are performing?

What if you don't already know what you're supposed to do, if you don't have a memory or dream you've been holding on to for the last fifteen or twenty years? How do you figure out your purpose in life?

I would suggest that you let go of any pressure or fear and remind yourself that it's not something to worry about. Just keep doing what you're doing. Continue to go through the 5 Steps of Slow Living and work through the steps in each portion of the Peace Pyramid.

The good news is that if you are in this section of the pyramid, you already have a solid plan in place to live a lovely and wonderful life.

You have a good grasp of time management, your health and finances are in good working order, you know where the stapler lives in your home, and you have relationships that make you feel nurtured and cared for.

And that's more than most!

So please don't beat yourself up if you don't have any grand ideas that make you feel like you have a huge pull to get out of bed every morning. Sometimes you have to get out of bed in the morning to feed the cat.

Continue to trust that life is filled with lots of moving parts. You may not know how they all fit together for quite a while—and that's okay! Many times people write to me and confess that even though they reached a certain milestone birthday, they don't feel any different than they did in their early twenties, and they thought they'd be more "enlightened" or "wise" in their advanced years.

That's okay, too. You don't have to have it all figured out yet. Keep plodding forward. Remember, we are not heading to any particular destination point. Maybe you've gone through the 5 Steps to Slow Living and applied them to the foundational parts of the Peace Pyramid and have the thought: *Now what?*

Here's what: Give yourself a hug. Relish in the accomplishment that you have achieved by taking the time to examine all aspects of your life and consider yourself lucky: you're not dead yet!

Go back to the beginning with a new lens and begin inserting fun, whimsy, excitement, and joy into your Peace Pyramid.

If we apply the Mindset + Action + Consistency = Success formula to the feeling of peace and tranquility in your life, it might look a little like this:

Mindset: *What do I want to do every day? How do I want others to remember me?*

Action: *Begin to schedule chunks of time into your schedule for things that excite you and bring you joy.*

Consistency: *You're not a spreadsheet and can't expect that your life will resemble one. Revisit your dreams and goals on a seasonal basis and see if they still feel in alignment, and readjust as necessary.*

In the fourth and final part of the book, we are going to talk about putting all of this together in a way to help you make forward progress that feels steady and sustainable. Hang in there; you're doing great, and the progress *will* come!

# Part 4

# Walking It Out: The Journey

"Never underestimate the power you have
to take your life in a new direction."
—Germany Kent

You've made it to the last section of the book! Congratulations on getting this far! In the first part, we discussed what Slow Living is and how it can be beneficial to you as you go through life. In the second and third parts, I explained exactly how to go about mapping your life in all its key areas and how the different components of the Peace Pyramid (Time Management, Health, Finances, Organization, Relationships) are necessary to live a successful and sustainable life.

In this part, we will put everything together in a very practical way.

Before we begin, please remember that you are *not* behind. We all have different socioeconomic upbringings, cultures, religious beliefs, and past events.

Some of your past events may be hindering you from moving forward—only you know this about yourself. There isn't anything wrong with you if you have had occurrences that you can't move through on your own. If you feel that this may be the case, please reach out to your doctor and consider therapy to try and heal your past. That said, not everyone needs to fully heal their past in order to move forward, because everyone metabolizes trauma differently.

Remember that we are all about being intentionally SLOW, and I'd like for you to look within to see if you are ready to put an action plan together. This is about playing the best Game of Life you can with the cards and game pieces you were dealt.

Regardless of what you may have been taught or read in a book, I don't want you to think that you have "attracted" unpleasant things into your life because you thought bad thoughts. I think we can all agree that childhood abuse, natural disasters, disease, and horrific accidents unfortunately occur every day and have nothing to do with your thoughts.

Instead, I'd like you to focus only on the Here and Now and how you can begin implementing the 5 Steps to Slow Living in each of the sections of the Peace Pyramid.

This is how to build a strong, stable, and sustainable life that fulfills you and brings you joy and a sense of purpose.

# Chapter 14

# Your Blueprint for Achievement: The Three-Part Success Formula

"Small disciplines repeated with
consistency every day lead to great
achievements gained slowly over time."
—John C. Maxwell

You've worked through the three prior sections on mindset, action, and consistency. What happens when you put all the pieces together?

Success.

Some people look for external markers of success such as awards, trophies, or fancy cars. If you've read this far, I'd imagine you've already realized that such trivialities are not the marker of a life well-lived. Instead, I'd like you to really go within and poke at what success looks like for you.

For many, it boils down to *change*. When you do the exercises outlined in this book, you will have created lifelong change, because this is not a quick-fix or crash-diet formula.

Whenever you have an idea to make a change for the better, the idea part is Mindset. You also may have noticed that I cautiously suggest for you to "be in a good mood" when you make any sort of plan for yourself.

The same way you shouldn't commit to a new hairstyle when you're feeling discouraged or cranky, you should try not to make life-altering plans when you aren't in a good headspace.

Action is what you do to bring your plans to life. Most people spend the majority of their time in this state of Action.

Consistency is what you do on a regular basis with your Action steps to bring your vision to life. Let's look at a very typical goal as an example of how to use Mindset + Action + Consistency effectively.

We'll use losing weight as an example. Many people have the idea to lose weight at the beginning of the New Year, but statistically only 9 percent of those who commit to this resolution follow through.

This is because most people who make a plan for themselves try to "Action" their way to success instead of using the Mindset + Action + Consistency formula.

If you have an idea to lose weight by walking 10,000 steps a day, drinking 60 ounces of water, and eating low-carb foods, this sounds like a very sensible plan. This is Mindset. When you were calm and thoughtful, you came up with this idea.

If after a few days, the scale hasn't budged, and you begin to feel discouraged and disheartened, what do you do?

If you're like most people, you decide to switch up the Action. Maybe you think to yourself, *This isn't working*, so you switch from low-carb to low-calorie food choices.

Or you begin drinking protein shakes instead of water. Or perhaps instead of walking 10,000 steps a day, you join a gym and begin taking kickboxing lessons.

Sound familiar? Because you have now switched the variables, it's really hard to track whether or not this new Action is better, and if you are like most, you feel even more discouraged and would rather give up than continue having defeated thoughts such as, *It doesn't matter what I do, nothing works.*

You can't Action your way to success.

That statement goes against a huge body of advice doled out through the past few generations, when we were taught to work as hard as we can, for as long as we can, and expect that success would inevitably follow.

Nick Srnicek, co-author of the book *After Work: A History of the Home and the Fight for Free Time,* shared with the BBC that Hustle Culture dominated the early days of Silicon Valley due to competition to win funding from venture capitalists. This 24/7 work environment legitimized the idea that to be successful and get anything meaningful done, you have to put in long hours. Srnicek shared, "Hustle Culture ideology says that people are overworked not because they are economically driven to [over-work], but simply because this is the way go-getters get what they want."[30]

This isn't to say that you can't be a go-getter. I want for you to meet and exceed all of your personal and professional goals, but in a way that feels good and doesn't result in burnout.

# When You Get Discouraged

So let's utilize the Mindset + Action + Consistency formula with the weight loss example.

When you begin to feel discouraged that you aren't seeing the results you imagined as quickly as you'd like, stop. Don't take any further action.

Instead, go back and work on your mindset. It doesn't feel good to take action when you're feeling down or in a funk.

Do the things that you've learned, from experience, help put you in a better frame of mind. I like to journal, go on a long walk, take a nap, or do a bit of yoga. Some people that I've worked with like to read books, engage in crafts, garden, pray, or watch a movie.

If you'd like to use a guided journaling worksheet to help reset your mindset, I have one that you can download to use throughout the day at stephanieodea.com/daily.

Once you've found that you are in a better frame of mind, it's easier to stay consistent with your planned course of Action. If you need inspiration on what that may look like, the second and third parts of this book are dedicated to how to create a slow, steady, and sustainable action plan.

Once you have a plan in place, stick with it and don't change the variables until you've met a predetermined amount of time; I recommend thirty days as a first target milestone. This is what consistency looks like:

Mindset + Action + Consistency.

You can apply this formula to each part of the Peace Pyramid to see where you may be holding yourself back. The following example may help as you plan:

|  | **Mindset** | **Action** | **Consistency** |
|---|---|---|---|
| **Time Manage-ment** | More free time | Get up earlier | Set alarm for 5 a.m. |
| **Health** | Lower blood pressure | Go on more walks | Walk around block at lunchtime |
| **Finances** | Save for retirement | Transfer savings into investments | Set up auto-draft transfers |
| **Organiza-tion** | More orderly garage space | Clear shelves of boxes | Go through one box a week |
| **Relation-ships** | Find more friends | Join neighborhood volunteer group | Go to monthly meetings and engage |
| **Signs of Peace** | Feel calmer | Not getting mad at coworkers | Listening more than I speak |

## Manifestation and Magical Thinking

Sometimes people think that if they think or daydream a certain way, they'll be able to control the outcomes of their lives. As mentioned in the first part of this book, believing in a higher power or being spiritual is not something to be discouraged.

I absolutely believe in a higher power, and I find great comfort in my belief. But I also know that I have to do my part if I want to make progress toward my personal and professional goals. I grew up with the maxim "God helps those who help themselves" and still use it to nudge myself into action when I find that I'm sitting around and waiting for divine action to intervene.

As we go through the following exercises to break your really-big-dream life goals into bite-sized pieces, I'd like you to focus on the things that you can do all on your own, and then trust that God or the Universe will meet you halfway.

## SMART Goals Are Stupid

If you've been in the corporate world, you've likely heard of SMART goals—Specific, Measurable, Achievable, Relevant, Time-Bound.

The idea is that when you define these parameters as they pertain to your long-term corporate or business goals, they help ensure that your objectives are attainable within a certain timeframe.

The issue is that most people don't run their lives the way a corporation does.

In real life, you have variables you can't control, like other people, the weather, and spotty Wi-Fi. It can feel really discouraging to map out goals in this way and watch deadlines come and go if you need to put everything on hold to care for an elderly family member or pay for a roof that blew off in a recent storm.

Although I really love acronyms, I hate SMART goals and find them to be rather stupid when it comes to meeting your long-term goals in a sustainable way. This is usually because in order to track and prove that you've met the set goals, you'd have to follow a path laid out by someone else, instead of going within to follow your own ideas, instincts, whims, and moods.

Life is meant to be enjoyed, and if you aren't able to consistently and precisely always show growth, it does not mean you have failed or that you aren't doing it right. Because of this, I joked on a call once that I should make up an acronym for STUPID goals, so I did:

**S**top
**T**rusting
**U**nqualified
**P**eople
**I**n your
**D**ecisions

If you have an idea to do something monumental, and it's the type of idea or dream that can't be measured with a line graph or by showcasing constant growth, it doesn't mean that you should give up on your dream.

There are many well-meaning people you'll come across through the course of your life who will not leave the safety of their couch but who may feel warranted in doling out life advice. Don't let people who have not already done what you want to do hold you back from making progress.

In a frequently quoted TED Talk, "The Power of Vulnerability," author Brené Brown alluded to Teddy Roosevelt's inspiring "The Man in the Arena" speech, saying, "There are a million cheap seats in the world today filled with people who will never be brave with their own lives, but will spend every ounce of energy they have hurling advice and judgment at those of us trying to dare greatly. Their only contributions are criticism, cynicism, and fear-mongering. If you're criticizing from a place where you're not also putting yourself on the line, I'm not interested in your feedback."[31]

That is such good insight, and today is the best day to start putting it into practice.

So if you have an idea to write a book, begin an online business, invent the next life-changing gadget, or achieve any other ambitious dream—go for it. The stops and starts you have as you inch toward the end goal may not look like much to an outsider peering in, but I'd like for you to keep inching forward nonetheless.

With the right Mindset, a thoughtful plan of Action, and a commitment to Consistency, you will be well on your way to the kind of Success that brings greater peace, joy, and meaning to life.

# Chapter 15

# Preparing to Thrive: Your Three-Year Plan

"If you don't design your own life plan, chances are, you'll fall into someone else's plan. And guess what they have planned for you? Not much."
—Jim Rohn

While we can chart the progress of Slow Living almost immediately and start seeing benefits early in the process, if you want to completely transform your life in all areas of the Peace Pyramid, it will take you roughly three years.

Three years may sound like an awfully long time, but remember, we are going to do this in a way that doesn't create undue stress on your body or relationships or have you go into debt.

When I was younger, I made five-year plans for myself. Many people do this, and it makes a lot of sense. What I've found, however, is that once you hit adulthood, the years all sort of blend together and it's really difficult to take baby steps toward a goal or idea that seems so far away.

I'm a huge fan of New Year's resolutions, but if your goal is to completely transform or uplevel your life, one year isn't long enough. You'll feel rushed and end up taking shortcuts in one or more areas of the Peace Pyramid.

Three years is the sweet spot.

When we moved into the house previous to the one in which we live now, I wanted some privacy in the backyard while my young children were playing. I began researching fast-growing vines and learned that master gardeners have this saying when planting trees or vines:

- The first year it sleeps
- The second year it creeps
- The third year it leaps

I saw this firsthand with my own backyard vines. I continued to water and fertilize them, but I really couldn't tell that they were thriving because all of the growth happened under the soil. Right when I began to get frustrated that they weren't growing, I began to see some tendrils poke out from the stem. The next year the trunk thickened and branches began sprouting from all directions and the vine flourished on the trellis I'd nailed to the fence boards.

We have since moved from that house, but I still walk by often and can see that not only is the vine thriving, it's now actually stronger than the fence it originally needed for support!

This is exactly what it looks like when lasting change occurs. You may not notice from one day to the next that change is happening, but when you put it all together you'll see sweeping transformations in all aspects of your life.

# Get Out of the Passenger Seat

Beth was a coaching client of mine. We worked together for only a few weeks during the pandemic. She used the lockdown time to create a plan to better herself in all areas of the Peace Pyramid. You can hear her talk about her transformation in episodes 35 and 105 of the *Slow Living* podcast.

Beth was divorced and the single mom of a high schooler when she reached out. She didn't particularly love her day job, wanted to lose weight, had trouble creating and sticking to boundaries in her relationships, was looking to shore up her finances, and longed to feel more in control of her life.

In a nutshell, Beth wanted to climb out of the passenger seat and into the driver's seat for the remaining years of her life. Together, we mapped out a three-year plan, and Beth got to work. A few months shy of three years, Beth reported back to me:

> This past month I filed a petition to run for mayor of my little village on the November ballot. Our hope is to create an all-new ambulance service to include full-time paid EMTs. I have a lot of my heart invested in this election. My daughter, who is months away from her 20th birthday, has moved in with her boyfriend and I see her pretty regularly. This Saturday we stopped at a local orchard that had cut-your-own sunflowers and made bouquets, so much fun!
>
> Other news: my boyfriend has moved in with me, into my house in my little village. There were some improvements made to the house which made sense

to do before his belongings were brought in and now things are all set and settled. He's such a good guy with a good heart and we make each other laugh! I have now fallen in love with my day job and coworkers. My finances are in the best shape they've ever been in and I'm addressing an iron issue with my health. My pyramid is solid, Steph!

I love hearing good news like that! This is the exercise I had Beth complete during our time together:

|  | Where Am I Now? | Where Do I Want to Be? | What's in the Way? |
|---|---|---|---|
| Time Management |  |  |  |
| Health |  |  |  |
| Finances |  |  |  |
| Organization |  |  |  |
| Relationships |  |  |  |
| Signs of Peace |  |  |  |

Once you know where you're headed and what's in the way of getting there, you can plot out the action steps to take on a regular basis. This is why I really encourage you to take the time to write out your three-year plan.

It might help you to begin with these questions: If you had a magic wand and all was amazing in each area of the Peace Pyramid, what would it look like? To get from where you are to where you want to go, what is in the way?

## New Year's *Focus*

Once you have a vision of where you'd like your life to be in three years, you can break it down into manageable steps. I love the quip we were taught as a child on how to go about eating an elephant—one bite at a time.

Many people have a theme or focal point for each calendar year. This is different than a New Year's resolution because you're deciding to filter all of your decisions through this one focal point. For instance, if you wanted your yearly theme to be "Fun," you'd find a way to incorporate more fun into all aspects of your life and would begin to plan your months, weeks, and days to involve activities that you deem fun and enjoyable.

I use the following acronym for FOCUS:

**F**ollow
**O**ne
**C**ourse (of Action)
**U**ntil
**S**uccess

## 30-Day Challenges

Once you decide on your theme for the year, break it down even further with a handful of 30-Day Challenges.

Bonnie, a receptionist in a dental office, worked with me to come up with a few monthly challenges to help her meet her New Year's focus of All Things Health. She wanted to lose roughly forty pounds before her daughter got married (the wedding was two years away) and become a healthier person in the process. She had crash-dieted before but never had a sustainable approach to health and fitness.

Because of a past eating disorder, she didn't want to track calories or weigh herself. After proclaiming that her focus on the next year was "Health," we came up with the following plan:

- January: get up at 5 a.m.
- February: take 10k steps a day, get up at 5 a.m.
- March: drink 60 ounces water, 10k steps, get up at 5 a.m.
- April: 10 minutes yoga, 60 ounces water, 10k steps, get up at 5 a.m.
- May: lift weights in garage, 10 minutes yoga, 60 ounces water, 10k steps, get up at 5 a.m.
- June: increase protein, lift weights in garage, 10 minutes yoga, 60 ounces water, 10k steps, get up at 5 a.m.
- July–December: MAINTAIN

As you can see, we broke down the steps into bite-sized chunks and turned them into 30-Day Challenges.

What is great about this is that it follows the FOCUS acronym of Following One Course (of Action) Until Success: we didn't add a new thing to do until she was already successful in the previous element.

These challenges don't need to correspond to a month of the year, although they certainly can. It also isn't necessary that the 30-Day Challenges only take thirty days—just that you complete them. You can absolutely make forward progress toward your long-term goal if a 30-Day Challenge takes forty-five days to complete. That's just fine and you have not failed in any way if you decide or need to take a day off.

Bonnie reported back through an email message that her plan worked and that she was thrilled with the way she looked and felt in her mother-of-the-bride dress!

## Weekly Planning

At the beginning of each new week, take a look at your calendar. If you see things coming up that you need to prepare for, schedule in time to do so. For instance, if I see that on Wednesday at 7 a.m. I have a coaching call, I will ensure that at some point on Tuesday I have at least thirty minutes set aside to prepare for the call. If a family member's birthday is coming up, decide which day you'll shop for the present and schedule it in a time slot on your calendar. If you find that you have more things to do than time allows, see what items can be removed from your calendar or delegated to others.

## Daily Calendar

In Chapter 4, I shared that because I have a background in child development and psychology and used to run preschool centers, I like to set up my day similar to the way schools are run. Your daily calendar is the most important planning tool you'll use on a day-to-day basis.

When you have to do something, schedule it and assign it a date and time within your calendar. For example, if you know that you need to call the vet to set up an appointment, place the five-minute phone call on your calendar.

Get your to-do list out of your head and onto your calendar. When you do this, you immediately assign a start and end time to the task at hand, which will help keep you focused. Not all projects will be finished once you begin, and you'll probably need to continuously schedule in time to revisit them.

The same way a teacher can't expect a student to complete an entire math textbook within the allotted math period, you can't expect to finish each project you begin each day. That's okay; just schedule another time period into your daily calendar on another day.

## Habits

Incorporating one change or challenge at a time and then adding a new one is called Habit Stacking. James Clear writes in his book *Atomic Habits*, "When it comes to building new habits, you can use the connectedness of behavior to your advantage. One of the best ways to build a new habit is to identify a current habit you already do each day and then stack your new behavior on top."[32]

What's fun about Habit Stacking is that after a while it becomes muscle memory, and you no longer need to think about what the new habit is, because you just sort of launch into it while doing something else already.

For instance, I take forever to drink my morning cup of coffee, which means I pop it into the microwave four to five times each morning and set the timer for thirty seconds. I already have this slow-drinking coffee habit, and since I know this about myself, I now use those thirty seconds to do push-ups off the countertop in my kitchen.

My husband does a similar thing each morning. The water heater for our home is downstairs, in the garage, and it takes a while for the hot water to travel up the pipes to the master bathroom. He uses the time it takes for the water to warm up to do a set of sit-ups on the floor of the bathroom, and then steps into the shower.

If you are trying to remember to take vitamins or supplements before bed, put them near your toothbrush so you see them each time you go to brush your teeth.

The reason the 30-Day Challenges work better than a huge overhaul is because they are divided up and once the first new habit is developed, you can add to it without having to remember to do too many new things all at once.

After a while, your body springs into action through muscle memory. Just this past week, I needed to set an alarm for 3:20 a.m. to deliver my daughter to the airport for an international flight. Because I have such a well-ingrained morning routine, I popped out of bed, turned off my alarm, said to myself, "Today is the day that the Lord has made," walked down the stairs, put on coffee to brew, and then went back upstairs to gather laundry from all of the bathrooms.

I plopped the laundry in the machine, did a few countertop push-ups, watered the plant in the dining room (because it was Wednesday), and gathered my car keys and wallet, which were exactly where I always leave them: in a decorative bowl on the side table by the front door. I was ready to drive to the airport within ten minutes of rising and had already completed a few of my household chores!

## Don't Fake It Till You Make It

I've never been a fan of the notion to "fake your way to success," and it's not something I advise. When you're trying something new, you are not experienced nor are you an expert. And that's alright!

Don't pretend to be something that you're not. The advice of "fake it till you make it" will inevitably backfire because your brain will know that you are lying, and you'll be going against your natural instincts. Instead, honor your feelings of insecurity and try to learn and get better as you move forward.

No one expects you to understand something fully and completely if you're attempting it for the very first time.

This is also a great way to keep your identity and integrity in alignment. If you know, deep down inside, that your actions don't match the thoughts in your brain, you'll feel as if you are lying—and that doesn't feel good.

I was once asked by a television producer to look directly into a camera and say, "Wow, this is the best beef stew I ever had!" I'm not an actor, and I didn't want to say that line because, to me, all beef stew tastes the same.

"Oh, I can't say that," I responded.

"Sure you can!" he said. "It's right there in the teleprompter!"

I ended up switching the line to, "This sure is tasty stew!" which felt better and more honest.

When you consistently dismiss the little voices in your head that caution you from moving too fast or taking action that isn't lined up with your ethics, morals, and integrity, you risk letting your ego get too big.

In psychology, the ego can be defined as the part of the psyche responsible for our sense of self and our ability to interact with the outside world. It is generally thought to be the part of the self most closely connected to reality.

In today's society, when one is described as having a "big ego," it implies that they are preoccupied with their own importance and think they are better than others. Having a big ego is also often associated with narcissistic tendencies, a superiority complex, and being self-absorbed.

Author and spiritual leader Wayne Dyer uses the acronym EGO (Edging God Out) when describing having a "big ego."[33] I like this term because it quickly puts me in check if I think I'm becoming too pushy or self-righteous in my thoughts, writing, or teachings.

No one has all of the answers.

You are your own best expert of what will work and what won't in your life. When you are comfortable taking forward action in a new job or life experience, you may feel appropriately nervous or anxious, but you won't feel like you are lying or dismissing your natural instincts.

## Work-Life Balance

Work-life balance is about finding a healthy equilibrium between your job and personal life by ensuring that neither overwhelms the other.

This means dedicating time and energy to your work responsibilities while also making room for your personal interests, family, relaxation, and self-care.

It's definitely easier said than done, and there's no right or wrong way to achieve this.

According to a poll taken by Statista.com, an online platform that specializes in data gathering and visualization, 72 percent of those currently seeking employment put work-life balance at the top of their list when it comes to choosing careers.

Yet 48 percent of the same people self-describe as "workaholics," believe work-life balance is a myth, and think it's unachievable for them.[34]

I often get asked if work-life balance is possible, or if it's merely a myth. My simple answer is that you absolutely *can* find a system that works well for you and your family. But your system needs to be *your* system. Anyone who tells you that there is only one way to achieve balance or that it needs to look a certain way or you're doing it wrong is trying to sell you something.

That's why the main purpose of this book is to help you get from where you are to where you want to go in a slow, steady, personal, and sustainable way.

One of my daughters was a competitive gymnast for many years. A balance beam is only four inches wide, and it's quite tricky to walk from one end to the other without falling off. Many people envision a balance beam or a tightrope when they think about work-life balance. That's where the mistake lies, because it insinuates that the only way to get to the other end without falling off is to do it very, very carefully ("perfectly") with no wobbles.

*No.* You can get to the other end by climbing off the balance beam and merely walking on the ground. Slow Down. Simply Look Only Within.

Ask yourself, *What would work-life balance look like for me?*

Then go quiet and listen to what bubbles up. It may mean that you need to get up a bit earlier in the morning so you don't feel rushed as you're getting ready for work. It may mean that you schedule grocery deliveries or begin carpooling for soccer practice. Maybe it means that you keep workout clothes in the trunk of your car and hit the gym on the way home from work.

Only *you* know what will work and not work for you and your family. No one but you will know what is happening in your home, your life, your brain, and your body.

# Chapter 16

# Savor Every Day: Enjoying the Journey

"Success is a journey, not a
destination. The doing is often
more important than the outcome."
—Arthur Ashe

When you are working toward long-term goals, sometimes it's hard to remember to enjoy the journey. For a good portion of my adult life, I felt as if I had to constantly be in motion or be productive in order to "earn" rest.

I don't want you to feel this way. It's not a fun feeling. I had the idea that instead of enjoying three-day weekends when they turned up on the calendar, I used them as a way to "squeeze in" extra work. In fact, I remember muttering to myself as I ripped up the backyard one year, "Well, they don't call it LABOR Day for nothing!"

This is because I only felt successful and purposeful when I was *doing* something and viewed resting and relaxing as a "reward," not a basic human right.

I'd also sometimes tell myself that I would "have fun when the work is done," but since I am a goal-oriented, somewhat Type A, driven person, the work is never done.

That's part of living. You'll always be working toward something, and that is what gets you up and out of bed in the morning. But don't forget to enjoy the process. Celebrate milestones along the way and savor the Here and Now as much as you can. Having fun and collecting memories is what makes a long life enjoyable.

You also may need to shift your mindset to one where you're okay with taking time off and fully relaxing. Productivity does not equal worthiness.

If you can't find a way to relax and feel good about stopping, slowing down, and resting, perhaps check in with your doctor. Feeling as if you aren't making progress unless you're in "overdrive" isn't sustainable for long-term success.

## Running a Very Long Marathon

In 2008, I signed up for and completed a half-marathon (13.1 miles) in San Francisco. I thought the route over the Golden Gate Bridge and through the park sounded lovely, my husband was already signed up, and I wanted to challenge myself.

Also, I wanted to take a photo of myself soaking my feet in a slow cooker at the end of the race and post it online.

I did all these things, and while I was running the streets of San Francisco, I remember chanting to myself, "One foot in front of the other, Steph. That's all you have to do." San Francisco has a *lot* of hills. It would have been a ton easier to run 13.1 miles on flat roads, but I didn't have a choice.

In life, just like when you're running, sometimes you have to exert yourself more than you'd prefer to get to the next location. The energy you'll need to muster to get up a long and winding hill is similar to the energy you'll need to engage during a busy season at work, or while in the midst of moving homes, or while caring for a newborn baby.

This isn't sustainable energy, but usually people can fight through the discomfort because they understand that there is an end in sight.

I am currently living in an unsustainable way while writing the draft of this book. When I have a strict writing deadline, I become an insomniac. It's easier for me to get up in the middle of the night and write when the house is quiet and I'm alone with my thoughts and the coffee pot than it is for me to try to be creative during daylight hours when I can easily become distracted.

My brain becomes busy and buzzy when I'm in "writing mode," and since I can't turn it off without the use of medication, I've decided to embrace it and use the quiet, middle-of-the-night hours to write. This works for me in short bursts of about six weeks, but it isn't a sustainable way for me to live over the long haul.

Because I know this current stage requires more of my energy and can be draining in other areas of my life, I've tried to pay extra special attention to the sections of the Peace Pyramid so I can work through this spurt.

For instance, I created a six-week meal plan with an accompanying grocery list and delegated the grocery shopping to my husband and one of our daughters. I go to bed each night at about 7 p.m. I'm limiting sugar and alcohol in my diet because those foods deplete my energy and focus. I've found ways to nap each weekend day and take catnaps in the car during break times at work. I've heavily increased my water intake and have stopped partaking in strenuous exercise. I've also lessened how often I vacuum and run the laundry.

For this short burst of time, I've blocked off any early-morning meetings from my calendar and said "No, thank you" to weekend events that might interfere with napping.

I'm now at the tail end of my six-week stint and have accomplished what I set out to do. Because I took these necessary and precautionary measures, I feel fantastic and triumphant, instead of burned out.

If you don't have an end in sight, or you don't see a way to stop an unsustainable workload, please reevaluate if you can, and go back to Step 1 of the 5 Steps to Slow Living to see what you can offload or declutter.

My concern is that if you keep going at an unsustainable pace and don't rearrange your life to be simpler or less intense, your body will force it upon you.

## Give Yourself the Gold Stars

Because of my background in Early Childhood Education, I learned that the best way to get a room full of toddlers or preschoolers to follow classroom rules or reach new educational milestones was to reward them along the way with stickers on a chart. I find that when working with adults, many of us have an inner child that craves praise and rewards. I joke when a coaching client achieves a new milestone that I'm happy to dole out gold stars to them as a reward.

The newness that comes from a new job or a new relationship feels exciting and provides a sense of purpose and worthiness, especially if your new partner or work colleagues compliment and affirm you. Because of this, each new thing that you learn or uncover feels like a reward. In

2020, the American Physiological Society released research indicating that when a reward is given for performing a behavior, a tiny bit of dopamine is released, which triggers a positive response in the brain.

The issue is that, over time, the newness wears off and your brain is no longer stimulated by a burst of dopamine. My suggestion is then to find a way to reward yourself instead of looking for outside stimuli.[35]

If you are now in a place where you have the job, the marriage, the kids, the house, and you still aren't feeling satisfied, it's time to find a way to experience pleasure and reward in the mundane. You're in the marathon season of your life instead of the sprinting-toward-shiny-objects phase.

This is a good thing, and what so many are working toward!

## Being Bored

On a related note, after you've been an adult for a while and you seem to be moving steadily toward your long-term goals in a slow and sustainable way, life can sometimes feel a bit boring. This also is normal.

When you're young, you have huge milestones to rush toward such as graduation, starting a new relationship, combining lives, buying a home, having children, and more. But once you're in your mid-forties or so, things begin to feel a bit ho-hum. Again, this is normal.

But sometimes people get antsy because they can no longer count on the dopamine hit of energy and excitement from beginning new things. Unfortunately, many people begin to self-sabotage in this phase of their lives because they feel as if they don't have anything else to look forward to.

Don't let yourself get to the point where you begin to take for granted the things that you've worked so hard to achieve.

This may also be a good time to take a look at your life and see where you are having a hard time with PACE. In Part 1 of this book, which is all about Mindset and the definition of Slow Living, I introduced you to the acronym for PACE:

**P**eaceful
**A**cceptance of
**C**hanging
**E**vents

When you've worked long and hard to reach a certain stage of life and then find that the world, or your neighborhood, or your (family, work, body . . .) is changing, it can feel quite defeating.

Change is difficult even for the most enlightened, and it's especially difficult if you have not initiated this change and it instead was forced upon you. This can be a seemingly minor change such as the local playground turning into a parking lot, or it can be a rather large change such as being diagnosed with a life-altering medical condition.

In episode 102 of the *Slow Living* podcast,[36] my friend Angela joined me to talk about how her life trajectory completely pivoted when she learned she had Multiple Sclerosis as a new college graduate.

Angela is the first to declare that she would not wish anyone to have MS, but she also shared that she became determined to not let this diagnosis hold her back from living the life that she wanted to live.

She just needed to do so in a slightly different way to honor her body and its needs. I call this going to "And Land."

This is tricky because, for most of us, we allow obstacles to throw us completely off our path. Instead of living in And Land, we get stuck in the Land of Either/Or.

If you live in the Land of Either/Or, you may have the following thoughts:

- *I can be a fun mom OR I could have a clean kitchen.*
- *I can get up early to work out OR I could get a good night's sleep.*
- *I can eat salad OR I could eat a doughnut.*
- *I can make money OR I could help others.*
- *I can pay off my car loan OR I could save for college.*
- *I can lose weight OR I could eat out at a restaurant.*

The Land of Either/Or is not a fun place to be, and it's rather exhausting. This is because you're having little baby battles in your brain all day long. So let's change it. If you live in And Land, your thoughts may be something like these:

- *I can be a fun mom AND have a clutter-free home.*
- *I can have fibromyalgia AND walk every day.*
- *I can be a good Christian AND make money.*
- *I can be in the throes of perimenopause AND continue to lose weight.*
- *I can get up early to journal and meditate AND feel well-rested.*
- *I can go out with my friends AND stick to my eating plan.*

It's a very subtle shift in thinking, but if you allow yourself to embrace your inner three-year-old and instead of declaring, "No way, I can't do this," you begin asking, "How?" your brain will begin working on solving the problem and answering the question.

In school settings, we teach children to embrace a growth mindset, and Angela is a phenomenal example of someone who has done just that. Despite facing a life-altering diagnosis and enduring the painful realities of her condition, she adopted an And Land mindset and resolved to enjoy her journey despite its challenges.

The same can be true for me and for you. Whether we're running a half-marathon or running our kids to another practice after school, remember: it's not always the destination that makes life worth living; more often it's the peace and joy we discover along the way.

# Conclusion:
# Redefining Success

"It's high time to redefine success. Success
is not something that you reach—not
something that is outside of yourself,
just down the field. Success is creating a
life you want to live in right now."
—Erich Fromm

Melody reached out to me after taking my Simple Shortcuts to Peace course (available through my website).[37] She shared that she had met with a few different therapists over the course of her adult life, but each had declared that there wasn't anything wrong with her and that she didn't need therapy.

Yet she felt unsuccessful and ashamed because she hadn't met the goals she had laid out for herself at a young age.

After a few calls, it was revealed that Melody made a timeline for herself when she was fifteen that she would be married by twenty-five, have kids by thirty, and have a house by thirty-five.

She was now forty-one and wasn't married, didn't want to have kids, and preferred living in a small apartment so she could use her spending money for travel and eating out. She also shared with me that she was quite content and at peace with her life.

When I pressed to see what the problem was, she said she felt like she hadn't succeeded because she hadn't done any of the things she'd said she would when she was younger. I told her that it was okay to redefine her definition of success, and relief immediately washed over her face.

This happens to a lot of people, and it's something to pay attention to as you make your way through your life.

Success comes in all shapes and sizes and it doesn't only look a certain way. You get to decide what success looks like for you. If you don't feel successful right now, take a look at how you are defining it. You may need to do a bit of tweaking.

\* \* \*

In Part 1 of this book, I wrote about ANTs—Automatic Negative Thoughts that sometimes pop into our heads, and if we aren't careful, can lessen our self-esteem.

One of the best ways to help stamp out ANTs or unconscious negative beliefs is through affirmations.

Affirmations sometimes get a bad rap for being silly and nonsensical due to television sketches such as the one on *Saturday Night Live* of Stuart Smalley talking to himself in a mirror. If you haven't seen the clips, they're worth looking up on YouTube.[38] Stuart Smalley is a satirical, fictional character created and performed by comedian Al Franken. The character appears in a mock self-help show called *Daily Affirmations with Stuart Smalley*. It first aired in 1991 but has stuck in the back of many viewers' brains and led some to perceive that affirmations are hokey and not worthwhile.

*The Washington Post* critiqued the Stuart Smalley satirical approach to affirmations in May of 2022 in a well-researched article by Allyson Chiu. In it, Chiu quotes studies and scientists that say affirmations can produce a wide array of positive effects, such as higher self-esteem; lower stress and cortisol levels; and a higher rate of productivity, goal setting, and achieving.[39]

I first became aware of affirmations and their boost in positive self-image and esteem when I was working for a county social services agency and ran a preschool center for homeless children. In the staff room was a dog-eared *Inner Talk* catalog put out by Progressive Awareness.[40] I spent many coffee breaks looking through the offerings and, after a few months, decided to use my own money to order a CD of positive affirmations to play for my preschoolers during nap time.

The affirmations were cuddled in the sounds of ocean waves and said statements such as: *I am safe, I am secure, I am loved, I am worthy, I am good, I can learn hard things.*

I didn't know if the positive, affirming statements would help to change the life trajectory of the children in my care but figured they couldn't hurt. I also whispered these phrases into their ears as often as I could while they sat on my lap for story time or as I rubbed their backs while they fell asleep during their daily afternoon naps.

When I became a mother, I did something similar when my children were babies and tried to remember to give them boosts of self-esteem as often as I could, although I'm the first to admit that real life got in the way of my best intentions at times.

One of the days that I felt I was failing my kids is burned into my memory.

It was a super foggy San Francisco Bay Area day, and I vividly remember feeling rushed as I frantically tried to get my third grader and kindergartener to school before the bell rang and the morning Pledge of Allegiance assembly began outside on the blacktop.

I had my baby strapped to my chest in a sling, I was pulling my kindergartener up the hill toward the blacktop, and I'm pretty sure my third grader was on the verge of tears.

It was another morning when I felt stressed and overwhelmed and behind, and I'm certain I was yelling about something that really wasn't important at all.

I smoothed my eldest's hair back into place and rearranged her ponytail as she stood in line. I felt horrible for lashing out and was trying my hardest to keep it all together, even though I was terribly sleep-deprived, hormonal, and felt that I was falling behind in work.

Mr. Gallagher was a fifth-grade teacher at the school, and he was absolutely wonderful. He has since passed away, but he always had a calm force about him and commanded any space he entered. He made a concerted effort each morning to walk the line of students, shake each of their hands (firmly, with eye contact), and tell them "Good morning" by name. The students then replied, "Good morning, Mr. Gallagher."

Since I felt tremendously guilty for snapping at my kids, I was hanging around the line instead of leaving to congregate with the other parents. As Mr. Gallagher approached, I gave my eldest daughter one last squeeze and quickly murmured whatever words I could summon that might somehow soothe her upset-ness. I said, "I love you, I'm proud of you, and I think you are wonderful."

We hugged and I pulled away.

Mr. Gallagher stopped me. He said directly to me, "Those are wonderful sentiments, and you should tell your children that every single day."

It's been many years since that day, but I took his words to heart and have tried my hardest to tell each of my three children these words daily.

If you don't have a Mr. Gallagher in your life, or someone close to you who might tell you these things, allow me:

I love you.
I'm proud of you.
And I think you are wonderful.

Take the time to really absorb these words and feel them in your bones. Many people cry when I first ask them to meet their eyes in a mirror and state these words. If you aren't ready to look at yourself yet in the mirror, try writing the phrases down or saying them out loud.

My hope is that as you continue to go through the exercises in the previous pages, your self-esteem and self-confidence will soar and you'll realize that you are doing an amazing job and are on the way to building the life of your dreams.

Thank you for being here.

XOXO,

*Steph*

# Glossary of Acronyms

ANT: Automatic Negative Thoughts

DIET: Do I Eat This?

EGO: Edging God Out

FIBRE: Financial Independence Before Retiring Early

FIRE: Financial Independence Retire Early

FOCUS: Follow One Course (of Action) Until Success

FOMO: Figure Only Myself Out

HAES: Health At Every Size

NEAT: Non-Exercise Activity Thermogenesis

PACE: Peaceful Acceptance of Changing Events

PROM: Purge, Remove, Organize, Maintain

SLOW: Simply Look Only Within

SMART: Specific, Measurable, Achievable, Relevant, Time-bound

STUPID: Stop Trusting Unqualified People In (Your) Decisions

# Acknowledgments

Thank you to everyone who helped bring *Slow Living: Cultivating a Life of Purpose in a Hustle-Driven World* to life.

I definitely am not alone in bringing my dream to reality. I want to express my heartfelt appreciation to everyone who played a part in the making of this book.

Thank you to Meredith Ethington, author of *The Mother Load*, for introducing me to Dexterity Publishing, and my fabulous editors: Jennifer Gott, Elisa Stanford, and Phil Newman. Thank you also to founder Matt West, Ashley Harris, Emma Sherk, and everyone else on the Dexterity team.

My dear husband, Adam, thank you for your constant support, patience, and unconditional love as I hemmed and hawed for a good fifteen years about whether or not I should write this book.

My three children: Amanda, Molly, and Katie O'Dea—I am so proud of who you are and am thrilled to watch you grow and evolve as you navigate young adulthood. I appreciate you showing me that there is always another way to look at things and I appreciate you constantly keeping me humble.

My parents, Perky and Bill Ramroth, thank you so much for taking the time to read each and every word of my writing since kindergarten and for always being willing to be the first round of editing.

My brother and sister-in-law, Andy and Karen Ramroth, thanks for always cheering me on and for helping me streamline my ideas into those that are understandable and relatable. I greatly appreciate being able to bounce thoughts off of the two of you and learning new perspectives!

Thank you to Jennifer Bloom-Smith for spending twenty to thirty minutes on the phone each morning while I wrote this manuscript, and for being such a wonderful friend for nearly thirty years. You helped me stick to my writing schedule because I wanted to report back to you that I was making forward progress and make you proud.

I feel immensely lucky to have such an amazing behind-the-scenes team who help to keep my websites up-to-date and my podcast properly edited and social media channels fed: Jennette Fulda, Tara Green, Taylor Condon, and Aleks Milenkovic.

To all of my readers and podcast listeners—I say it often, and I truly believe it: I have the best readers and listeners of all time. Thank you for being an abundant supply of inspiration and support. I hope you consider yourself loved and hugged, and please know that I think you are absolutely wonderful.

# Notes

1. "Cision's Top 50 Food Blogs List Offers Appetizing Data On Tastemakers in Food and Dining Media," Cision, July 9, 2012, https://www.globenewswire.com/en/ news-release/2012/07/09/272996/13711/en/Cisions-Top-50-Food-Blogs-List-Offers-Appetizing-Data-on-Tastemakers-in-Food-and-Dining-Media.html/.

2. "Suicide," National Institute of Mental Health, last updated February 2024, https://www.nimh.nih.gov/ health/statistics/suicide/.

3. "Stress," NHS, https://www.nhs.uk/mental-health/ feelings-symptoms-behaviours/feelings-and-symptoms/ stress/.

4. "The Number One Habit To Develop In Order To Feel More Positive," *Amen Clinics*, August 16, 2016, https:// www.amenclinics.com/blog/number-one-habit-develop-order-feel-positive/.

5. Yasmin Anwar, "Emoji fans take heart: Scientists pinpoint 27 states of emotion," *UC Berkeley News*, September 6, 2017, https://news.berkeley.edu/2017/09/06/27-emotions/.

6. Maxwell Maltz, *Psycho-Cybernetics: Updated and Expanded* (New York: TarcherPerigee, 2015).

7. Maltz, *Psycho-Cybernetics*.

8. See Brené Brown, *The Gifts of Imperfection: Let Go of Who You Think You're Supposed to Be and Embrace Who You Are*

(Center City, MH: Hazelden Publishing, 2010), as well as other books and talks by Brown in which she explores this concept.

9. Ben Schreckinger, "The Home of FOMO," *Boston Magazine*, July 29, 2014, https://www.bostonmagazine.com/news/2014/07/29/fomo-history/.

10. Stephanie O'Dea, "A Year of Slow Cooking," *Rachael Ray*, October 21, 2012, https://www.rachaelrayshow.com/video/a-year-of-slow-cooking/.

11. Serena J. J. Dyer and Dr. Wayne Dyer, *Don't Die with Your Music Still in You* (Hay House, 2014).

12. Stephanie O'Dea, "Episode 37 of the Slow Living Podcast: Finding Your Purpose," *The Slow Living Podcast*, December 15, 2022, https://stephanieodea.com/2022/12/episode-37-of-the-slow-living-podcast-finding-your-purpose/.

13. It's worth mentioning that Marie Kondo herself has chosen to slow down a bit, in a good way, from her tidying ways now that she's a busy mom. She still advocates decluttering and organizing, but she has adjusted her teaching in light of new life priorities and demands. See Mary Yang, "Marie Kondo Revealed She's 'Kind of Given Up' on Being So Tidy. People Freaked out," NPR, January 29, 2023, https://www.npr.org/2023/01/29/1152149068/marie-kondo-revealed-shes-kind-of-given-up-on-being-so-tidy-people-freaked-out/.

14. Summer Allen, PhD, "The Science of Gratitude," Greater Good Science Center, May 2018, https://ggsc.berkeley.edu/images/uploads/GGSC-JTF_White_Paper-Gratitude-FINAL.pdf.

15. Thomas J. Stanley, *The Millionaire Next Door: The Surprising Secrets of America's Wealthy* (New York: Gallery Books, 1996).

16. Esther and Jerry Hicks, *Ask and It Is Given: Learning to Manifest Your Desires* (Hay House, 2004).

17. "Big Rocks," FranklinCovey, YouTube.com, April 24, 2017, https://www.youtube.com/watch?v=zV3gMTOEWt8/.

18. "Health at Every Size," *National Geographic*, https://education.nationalgeographic.org/resource/health-every-size/.

19. "Physical Activity for Adults: An Overview," CDC, December 20, 2023, https://www.cdc.gov/physical-activity-basics/guidelines/adults.html/.

20. Christiaan G. Abildso, PhD, et al., "Prevalence of Meeting Aerobic, Muscle-Strengthening, and Combined Physical Activity Guidelines During Leisure Time Among Adults, by Rural-Urban Classification and Region—United States, 2020," CDC *Morbidity and Mortality Weekly Report*, January 27, 2023 / 72(4); 85–89, https://www.cdc.gov/mmwr/volumes/72/wr/mm7204a1.htm?s_cid=mm7204a1_w/.

21. "What Is PMDD?," IAPMD, https://iapmd.org/about-pmdd/.

22. "Suicide Statistics," American Foundation for Suicide Prevention, accessed May 11, 2024, https://afsp.org/suicide-statistics/.

23. Financial Peace here is used in the general context of the Peace Pyramid and is not a reference to the Dave Ramsey resources of the same name.

24. "USDA Food Plans: Monthly Cost of Food Reports," USDA, https://www.fns.usda.gov/cnpp/usda-food-plans-cost-food-monthly-reports/.

25. Satu H. Woodland, PMHCNS-BC, APRN, "Clutter can cause stress and anxiety: clean up now," Hope Mental Health, https://www.hopementalhealth.com/blog/clutter-can-cause-stress-and-anxiety-clean-up-now/.

26. The subjects of the Grant Study at Harvard included John F. Kennedy.

27. John Bowlby and Mary Ainsworth Inge Bretherton, "The Origins of Attachment Theory," Department of Child and Family Studies University of Wisconsin–Madison, *American Psychological Association*, 1992.

28. Lindsay C. Gibson, PsyD, *Adult Children of Emotionally Immature Parents: How to Heal from Distant, Rejecting, or Self-Involved Parents* (New Harbinger Publications, 2015).

29. Carla Bimberg, "Unapologetically Myself (musings on self-confidence)," https://carlabirnberg.com/2013/11/14/unapologetically-myself-musings-on-self-confidence/.

30. Helen Hester and Nick Srnicek, *After Work: A History of the Home and the Fight for Free Time* (New York: Verso, 2023).

31. Brené Brown, "The Power of Vulnerability," TedxHouston, YouTube.com, https://www.ted.com/talks/brene_brown_the_power_of_vulnerability/; Theodore Roosevelt, "Citizenship in a Republic" (aka "The Man in the Arena"), April 23, 1910, Theodore Roosevelt Center at Dickinson State University, https://www.theodorerooseveltcenter.org/Learn-About-TR/TR-Encyclopedia/Culture-and-Society/Man-in-the-Arena/.

32. James Clear, *Atomic Habits: An Easy and Proven Way to Build Good Habits and Break Bad Ones* (New York: Penguin Random House, 2018), 74.

33. Dr. Wayne W. Dyer, *Inspiration: Your Ultimate Calling* (Hay House, 2006); see also: "The Ego Illusion," Wayne's Blog, https://www.drwaynedyer.com/blog/the-ego-illusion/.

34. "How would you currently describe your work-life boundaries?" *Statista*, October 26, 2023, https://www.statista.com/statistics/1401223/remote-workers-work-life-boundaries-worldwide/.

35. Allan R. Wang et al., "The role of dopamine in reward-related behavior: shining new light on an old debate," *Journal of Neurophysiology*, July 24, 2020, https://www.journals.physiology.org/doi/full/10.1152/jn.00323.2020/.

36. Stephanie O'Dea, "Episode 102 of the Slow Living Podcast: Living with Multiple Sclerosis," *The Slow Living Podcast*, September 20, 2023, https://www.stephanieodea.com/2023/09/episode-102-of-the-slow-living-podcast-living-with-multiple-sclerosis/.

37. Simple Shortcuts to Peace course, Stephanie O'Dea, https://www.stephanieodea.com/peace/.

38. One Stuart Smalley clip among many is "Daily Affirmation: Politics - Saturday Night Live," YouTube.com, September 23, 2013, https://www.youtube.com/watch?v=HMRX-Wj2WOk/.

39. Allyson Chiu, "How to Make Self-Affirmation Work, Based on Science," *Washington Post*, May 2, 2022, https://www.washingtonpost.com/wellness/2022/05/02/do-self-affirmations-work/.

40. "Innertalk: The Missing Pieces to the Success Puzzle," Progressive Awareness Research, Inc., January 2014, https://www.innertalk.com/Catalog-InnerTalk.pdf.

# About the Author

Stephanie O'Dea is a *New York Times* best-selling author, certified life coach, and podcast host. She holds a bachelor's in English Literature and an AA in Early Childhood Education. Before her writing career, Stephanie worked for the Family Service Agency of San Mateo County, California, where she ran preschool centers for underprivileged children. She also opened a childcare center for Shelter Network and established two drop-in childcare centers for the San Mateo County court system.

Stephanie gained widespread recognition for her blog *A Year of Slow Cooking*, where she fulfilled a New Year's resolution to use her slow cooker every day for a year and write about it online. Her work has been featured on numerous media platforms, including *Good Morning America*, *Rachael Ray*, and Oprah.com. In addition to her culinary expertise, Stephanie is passionate about time management and helping busy families create efficient, joyful routines. In 2021, she launched the *Slow Living* podcast, became a certified life coach, and now helps busy people meet their personal and professional goals.

She lives in the San Francisco Bay Area with her husband, their three daughters, and a basset hound named Sheldon.

Stephanie is also the author of:

*Make It Fast, Cook It Slow: The Big Book of Everyday Slow Cooking*

*More Make It Fast, Cook It Slow: 200 Brand-New, Budget-Friendly Slow Cooker Recipes*

*365 Slow Cooker Suppers*

*5 Ingredients or Less Slow Cooker Cookbook*

*Totally Together: Shortcuts to an Organized Life*

*Clean Less, Play More: Housekeeping for Normal People*

*2, 4, 6, EAT: Intermittent Fasting, Simplified*

*How to Live Slowly: Peaceful Serenity in a Frenzied World*

*30 Days to a New You: A Motivational Journal and Workbook*

*The Mommy Blogger Next Door: A.K.A. How I Became the CrockPot Lady*

You can find her online at StephanieODea.com.

Made in the USA
Middletown, DE
30 October 2024